Boso's Brother Dindi

Linda Harvey Kelley

To Gill + Sarah,

To Rock Lake
Camp:
Linda Harvey Kelley

Come + see me sometime in Greece!
God bless you in Kosovo
Linda Harvey Kelley

Linda Harvey Kelley
2016

DEDICATION

I dedicate this book to the memory of the great warrior, Mambi, who became a stalwart soldier for Christ. He was an honorable Christian gentleman with the ability to give a great compliment ~ the kind you could live on for months, as Mark Twain said.

And to the memory of his two sons, Carl Kanga Mambi and Jacob Walea Mambi ~ agents of change in the emerging nation of Papua New Guinea.

CONTENTS

ACKNOWLEDGMENTS

I must acknowledge Jack London's book of *Adventure*,
published 1911, which gave me the idea of writing
Anglicized Melanesian Pidgin, i.e. spelling it in the English
words from which it derives.
I acknowledge the word-of-mouth stories recounted in this
book, primarily by Carl Kanga Mambi, but also other
Katiloma people and Sugu Valley people. I acknowledge
my appreciation to all of them for telling me their history.

Linda Harvey Kelley

FOREWORD

A baby boy was born to Mambi and his youngest wife about 1958 or 1959, and though his mother died soon after he was born, he flourished under his brother's care. Kanga Mambi, aka Boso, was probably only about ten years old or less when he rescued his baby brother from the mother's grave. It was nearly ten years later when I arrived at Katiloma, and Kanga told me the story, again and again. By that time the little boy who had been given several different names during his short life, and had started "Prep" or kindergarten with the name Walea, was a student in Marilyn Lavy's third grade classroom, and had chosen the name Jacob for himself. I call him Dindi in this story; he wouldn't be Jacob for years yet.

Jacob was picking up English almost as fast as he had learned Melanesian Pidgin as a toddler. He was at the top of his class with three other boys, and as a reward for hundreds on an exam, Marilyn Lavy had told the four boys they could choose a Bible name and she would call them by their chosen name from then on in school. The boys chose Jacob, Joseph, Jesse and David, and those four were the only ones out of a class of forty who were allowed by the government to go to high school from that first sixth-grade class at Katiloma. They went on to Ialibu High School, and during that time, Jacob felt he had a call to preach, and the Kelleys assisted him in going to Adirondack Bible College in New York State, USA.

Ever a lover of languages, Jacob enjoyed learning Koine Greek, there in the mountains of New York, and as I was still in Papua New Guinea, and also loved Greek, he got in the habit of ending his letters to me and my family with a Greek sentence or paragraph at the end.

Unfortunately, just before his return to Papua New Guinea, Jacob's brother, Kanga/Carl Mambi, died of an aneurysm. By that time Kanga was married to Ruth Koya Mambi and had five children, David, Hannah, Daniel Daren and Donald.

Jacob returned to Katiloma where he preached for some time, took a wife from Ialibu, and took up life in Mendi as News Commentator and Translator for Radio Southern Highlands. He still holds this position in the Southern Highlands capitol. When I visited him in 2000 I took the pictures of him with his son, and his wife and two daughters in this book. He had written several poems and shared a couple of them with me. I include the one he wrote to me. Last year (2013) his firstborn daughter, Shalom Walea graduated from University of Papua New Guinea, and his second, Norah Shenandoah is still enrolled there.

In 2011, while I was visiting Papua New Guinea, Kanga's youngest son, police officer Donald Kanga Mambi was chopped by beer smugglers as he endeavored to do his duty. His body was washed down the Kaugel River where it was eaten by flesh-eating fish and eels. His bones and police uniform were retrieved at the mouth of the river a month later, and returned for burial to Katiloma. Jacob held wakes in Mendi and was not able to come out to Mt. Hagen to see me. He called me night after night, and we caught up on each other's lives and the lives of each other's children.

"Dear Linda"

Leaving snow-capped cities of the

Great Northern Lights, Past Ocean waves,

Across spanning sky ways, To the tropical

Isles of the South Seas, to climes unknown

And races untamed,

"How beautiful were your feet

That brought the Good News of Peace,"

Dear Linda.

Into foreign communes where everything was strange;

The chants and languages, beliefs and cultures, the

People and their life style, T'was a life of uncertainty,

Yet you identified so well culturally, spoke our
vernaculars,

Understood us so well, we treasure you,

Dear Linda.

You have helped shape the future of some of the
greatest

Men and women, like doctors, lawyers, leaders, etc. who

Now are at the helm of key government departments,

Making important decisions that would affect the future

Of this island nation,

With whom we treasure and admire you,

Dear Linda.

What other better time than now would you

Have chosen to come again, than to see the

First Mother's Day of the Millennium

In the land of your love and labors?

Oh, the care and concern you have shown

Goes beyond riches or fame and we promise

We will pray and have you in our hearts always,

And bon voyage, Dear Linda.

Jay Emm (J. M.) May 14, 2000

Linda Harvey Kelley and Jacob Mambi, aka Dindi,
read proof on this manuscript in 1992 at Kati-loma.

CHAPTER ONE: BATTLE

Boso wakened to the sound of men's voices. He crawled silently to the fireplace in the manhouse and wedged himself in between his Apa (papa) and Uncle Kira.

"How soon are you going, Apa?"

"Right away, my son. We're just putting some poison on these arrow tips. If we leave now we will reach the enemy before big-sun."

"I wish you wouldn't go," came a voice out of the darkness outside.

"Ama," said Boso, squinting his eyes to search the black outdoors for his mother.

"I have this intuition of danger. I have a premonition that you will be killed, Father of my sons. I wish you wouldn't go."

"And when would I ever go to battle if I listened to women's fears?" asked the great warrior, Mambi. "How would I have won this land we are living on right now, if I had stayed home every time a woman asked me?"

"But I have never asked you to stay home before. I have never had such a premonition before."

"Well, if it wasn't you, it was one of my other wives. How am I to keep track of which silly woman it was each time?"

"Hand me that arrow, Mambi. Then mine are done," said one of the men.

"Mine, too."

"So are mine," echoed other men.

The men crawled out of the manhouse, climbed over the pig barrier, and began to stretch and flex their muscles.

"*Kati! Kati*!" Someone began the war chant.

"O Father-of-my-sons-iyo –iyo –iyo," Boso's mother began to wail.

"Why must you rush to the spirit world? –iyo –iyo –iyo

"Why not be content with the land you have already won? –iyo –iyo –iyo   Father-of-my-sons, I will be mourning your death tonight. –iyo –iyo –iyo."

"Stop that infernal keening, woman! Men, let's go! *Kati! Kati! Kati! Kati*! Who's ready to fight?"

 "*Kati! Kati!*" returned the men as they accepted gifts of sweet potatoes from the women who were gathered around the manhouse. By the light of the manhouse porch fire, each woman found her man, to give him last-minute gifts of sweet potatoes, cooked bananas, and tasty mushrooms. Some women joined Boso's mother in the mourning chant.

"We'll be sitting here in the dirt crying, chanted Boso-Ma.

"Iyo –iyo –iyo –iyo –iyo," came the joint chorus from several women.

"You'll find us here, if any of you live to return, iyo –iyo –iyo –iyo."

"*Patepape!* Good-bye! Good-bye! We're off to fight! Kati! Kati! We're off to fight! Bring the pitpit torch, Kira!"

Boso stood with the crying women and watched until the men and the pitpit torch were out of sight.

"What do we do now, Boso?" asked Tikira, Boso's

older brother.

Boso was still thinking about his father, and his mother's premonition of danger. He gave no answer. Tikira grabbed his hand.

"Come on, Boso, let's go back to sleep."

Boso pulled his hand away and went and squatted beside his mother.

"Ama, do you have a sweet potato for me?"

She searched in her net-bag and drew out a sweet potato without missing a beat of her chant.

"For me too, Ama?" asked Tikira.

Both boys squatted on the cold, damp earth, until Ama's net-bag was empty. Tikira finished his last potato first. He got up and returned to the manhouse fire. Boso followed. Other boys sat around finishing off their mothers' store of cooked food. Some boys were already asleep by the fire. Boso and Tikira curled up as close as they could get to the manhouse fire, and fell asleep to the tune of their mother's mournful song.

The sun was shining brightly when Boso opened his eyes again. He sat up and adjusted his wide bark belt. He smoothed his rumpled tanket leaves over his hips, and centered his netting of bark thread in front.

"Hey, Tikira, let's go to Ama's garden and see if we can get any sugar cane. I am thirsty for sugar juice."

"Bet I can beat you there," said Tikira as he jumped the manhouse patio post, being careful not to bump his head on the pig jawbones hanging from the porch roof. Their tribe had killed one hundred five pigs, at the last pig feast, and the jawbones hung there as mute testimony of the tribe's wealth and generosity.

"No fair, Long Legs. I don't feel like running," Boso called to Tikira as the older boy topped the second hill. "I'm going to stop here for a drink, anyhow."

"Bet I'll have Ama's sugarcane gone before you get there!" taunted Tikira.

Boso ignored him as he walked around the little pole

bridge and scooped up water in his hands.

"Boso-yo!" called a woman's voice.

Boso stood up and scanned the hillside sweet potato garden bordering the creek.

"Nogo-Ma!" he shouted when he spotted his father's third wife, sitting among the sweet potato mounds, her brown body and green grass skirt the perfect camouflage against the brown earth and green leaves.

"Do I know a boy who is thirsty for sugar juice?"

"Yes, you do, and you're looking at him right now!" said Boso, glancing over his shoulder and up the hill to make sure his brother was out of sight. He hoped he was out of hearing as well.

"I've got a nice stick of sugarcane growing right here beside me. Come up and get it."

Boso picked his way through the mounds, stepping carefully only in the depressions where sweet potatoes were not growing.

He squatted in front of the pregnant woman who was busily uprooting sweet potatoes with her digging stick.

"Nogo-Ma, do you have any fears about Apa?"

Nogo-Ma stopped digging to look into the boy's worried eyes.

"No, Boso, your father is a great man. Tribes all around say he is indestructible. You know that."

"Yes, I know. But Ama had a premon-, a premonition that he might get killed."

"And you're afraid it is woman's intuition?

"Something like that. What would our tribe do without Apa? He's the greatest warrior the Kati-loma have."

"You're right. He's not only the greatest warrior. He is the greatest man I have ever known."

"You mean richest?"

"Well, that too, maybe. Although actually, I have known richer men. A man in my father's tribe had seven wives, and I've seen a man on the other side of Kagua who had ten wives. He also has enough pigs to buy five more

4

wives."

"And Apa has only five wives."

"Yes, I wasn't calling him great because of his riches. I meant great in character."

"How is his character great?"

"He is the kindest, wisest, most disciplined man I know."

"Disciplined? How do you mean?"

"He's self-controlled. He doesn't get furiously angry. Don't you know? He never beats us women or you children."

"That's true. I hadn't thought about it. Naki's father hit him over the head with the serving tongs last week and spilled his blood. Apa has never done that to me. But when he scolds me I feel so ashamed I wish I could crawl into a hole like a bandicoot or disappear into thin air like a ghost. You don't call that anger?"

"No, because he is not out of control. He's just trying to help you grow up right and be a great man like he is."

"You think that's his reason?"

"Of course."

"And he never beats any of his wives?"

"No, he never does. And he never kills any women or children in battle, either."

"You're right. I know that's true. Except for one time when he was real young. He killed a woman in the heat of battle, he says, and he has regretted it ever since, he says. He is even ashamed of it. But the other men in the *tapanda* (manhouse) tease him about his scruples. They say, 'Go ahead, save the young women for us, but kill the married women.' But Apa always says 'No'."

"Right. The fact that he has enough sense to be ashamed of his one indiscretion shows his wisdom and greatness. He's a great man, all right. And you're going to be like him."

"Me?"

"Yes, you."

"Why? How me?" Boso was so surprised he could not talk correctly.

"You're the greatest of his sons."

"How am I great?"

"You're a natural leader, just like your father. The boys always follow you in play. Haven't you noticed? Even Tikira, your older brother, follows you."

"Sometimes. Other times they are stubborn and won't follow the rules I make in our games and in our fights."

"Yes, but you usually find ways to talk them around, I've observed."

"Maybe so. I hadn't thought about it."

"This is deep thinking for a thirsty boy. I almost forgot about the sugar."

Nogo-Ma stood up with a little groan and broke him a tall stick of sugar cane.

"Thanks, Nogo-Ma."

She hunched down again, settling with a sigh, and patted her stomach.

"I hope this baby is a boy and that he will grow up to be great like his Apa and his brother, Boso."

"Like Apa, but not like me, Nogo-Ma. I am not disciplined like Apa is. I get so mad sometimes. And worse yet, I get so scared at night. Do you think Apa is ever afraid?"

"No, Boso, I don't think he is ever afraid. He is the bravest man I have ever known. How badly I have wanted to give him a son! A healthy boy to grow up strong and brave like him! But all three of my sons have died. Only my daughter, Nogo, has lived."

"Where is Nogo, by the way?"

"I told her to go find me some mushrooms. I am hungry for something besides sweet potatoes. I don't feel well and I am having a hard time making myself eat them. I wish I had some meat. I don't want to get too weak before the baby is born. If I don't eat enough, he might die. Oh, how I want to give your Apa a fine strong son!"

"I'll go hunting for you, Nogo-Ma! I was going anyway. But I will bring back my kill to you, and we will eat it together! I made myself a new bow last week and I am going to try it out today." He stood up. "I better go right away."

"Have another stick of sugar cane to take with you in case you get thirsty at *big-sun*."

"Which one?"

"Break that tallest one right there to your left."

"Thanks, Nogo-Ma. I will be back as soon as I can."

Boso ran back to the manhouse for his new bow. He grabbed up five arrows too. Dare he go alone on this hunt? He had first gone hunting many times with Apa or Uncle Kira or Kaisuwa (grandfather). Then he had become braver and gone with other boys, and last with Tikira alone. But if Tikira or the boys went along now they would have to have a share of the meat. How they would tease him if they knew he was going to divide his share with a woman! Especially a woman who was not even his mother! No, he had better go alone. Nogo-Ma said Apa was never afraid. He wanted to be a great man like Apa. No better time than now to start developing his courage!

He hurried down a trail in the opposite direction from the one he had taken earlier that morning. He knew where there was a nice big tree kangaroo. He had missed him about ten days earlier and that was when he had decided he needed to make a new bow. Boso walked for two hours in the big bush, far from huts or gardens, straight to the very tree where he had spotted this relative of the possum. He would not miss this time! He had to get meat for his friend and her baby ~ his new baby brother, maybe! Imagine a baby in the family! Oh, how he hoped it would be a boy! Naki's mother had a new baby boy, born last week.

Boso wondered why his mother didn't have another baby. He had been grown a big boy for a long time now. He had twelve second teeth and he had not nursed his mother since he had lost his first baby tooth. Why doesn't Ama have another baby? Does she think three is enough? His older sister was now a woman, and married to a husband two moons ago. And Tikira had such long legs!

He got the tree kangaroo with the first arrow. It dropped to the ground, still struggling. Grabbing up a stone, he knocked it on the head.

Wheeeee! It was a big one! What good eating! But he might as well hunt some more. It wasn't that much past *big-sun*. So Nogo-Ma thought he could become a great man. Boso pondered this surprising statement as he listened to the jungle sounds around him. Hopefully those birdcalls were all being made by real birds, and not by spirits or stonemen. He had never seen a stoneman, of course. No one saw a stoneman and lived. He recalled fearful tales he had heard of men who saw a stoneman looking at them from the bush, or rivers, or mountains, and soon died. Was it wise, he wondered, to come alone to the jungle just to try to prove a courage he did not have?

A bush rat ran past him, but not fast enough. His thoughts continued while he gutted and cleaned the rat and tree kangaroo. So Nogo-Ma thought he was a leader. She had been observing him and the boys at play. No wonder he liked her so much. She thought he was special. Even greater than his older brother, Tikira. Well, Tikira had longer legs so Boso did have to use his brains to outsmart him. And must be that showed talent. And leadership ability. Wow! Boso's bare bony rib cage began to swell with pride.

A cockatoo warned of his approach in time for Boso to get a four-pronged arrow ready. That was an easy shot. He could get tiny birds easily with his new bow. The cockatoo wasn't even a challenge. My, what a feast they would have!

He plucked the cockatoo carefully saving all the gorgeous white feathers, and especially the yellow tufts, for singsings and festivals. He put the plucked bird into his belt bag with the two animals. He wrapped wild banana leaves around them to protect them from the sun, and to hide them from greedy eyes. No one was getting a share of this kill but Nogo and her mother. He hoped Nogo had found lots of mushrooms and was gathering some bush spinach as well. Greens and mushrooms and meat! His mouth was watering and his tummy was growling.

The afternoon sky clouded over and a tropical shower began to beat down on the boy and his meat. He cut several big breadfruit leaves and pinned them to his kinky hair and net bag with twigs. They would protect him and his bag from the rain. He draped another leaf over his front netting. No good "rotting in the rain". His mother worked hard to gather the right kind of bark, shred it, spin it into thread and crochet it into net coverings for her sons, or net bags for all of them.

Even though it was raining, Boso circled around to approach Nogo-Ma's house from the least visible angle.

"I'm coming," he called out, before he reached the door.

Instantly Nogo stuck her head out the low doorway. "Ho, Boso, are you rotting in the rain?"

"No, you see, I got me some nice breadfruit leaf coverings. Did you find many mushrooms?" he asked as he stooped to crawl into this woman's abode.

"Yes, bagfuls. They're already cooking with greens in these bamboo. I see you found something!" she squealed, as he lowered his bag beside the open fireplace in the center of the grass and cane hut.

"Yes, a tree kangaroo, a bush rat, and a cockatoo."

"Wow! What a feast we will have!"

"A great hunter you are, our Boso!" said Nogo-Ma. "My mouth is watering already!"

She lifted burning embers in her tongs and set them aside, hollowing out three spots in which to place the leaf-wrapped meat. She laid each bundle in its hollow in the ashes, covered them over with ashes, and replaced the hot coals and burning embers over them. She added new sticks of firewood, and set the waist-high lengths of bamboo against the wood at the sides of the fire.

The woman reached for a baked sweet potato, slapped the ashes from it vigorously, and handed it to Boso.

"Mm, I am hungry!" admitted the proud hunter. "I'll only eat one or two though, just to stay me until the meat is done.

"Tell us all about your hunt," said Nogo-Ma as she relaxed by the fire.

Boso tried to keep his eyes on hers and avoid looking at her swollen stomach and breasts. He couldn't remember ever sitting this close to a pregnant woman since he was old enough to notice.

"It wasn't anything. I knew where the tree kangaroo lived. Tikira and I discovered him the last time we went hunting. But my bow wasn't strong enough. All my arrows fell short, and Tikira's bow wasn't much better."

"Did you make this fine bow all by yourself?" She fingered the smoothness of it as she spoke.

"No, *Kaisuwa* helped me. I told him how my arrows fell short of this big fellow and I asked him to help me cut the right kind of sapling and a big enough one to make a man's bow. He brought out this piece he had cut many moons ago and was allowing to season. He helped me shape it and then I sanded it for two days; first with a flint stone and then with nettle. Didn't I get it nice, though?"

"You certainly did! How long have you been going on hunts alone?"

"Not long." Boso ducked his head, unwilling to admit this was the very first time. Under lowered brows he watched Nogo-Ma turn the bamboo containers.

"Will Tikira be mad that you went back and got this prize without him?" asked his half-sister.

"Yes, he will be mad if he finds out, but I won't tell him. A fellow has to learn some cunning in this world if he wants to get ahead." Boso snuck a look at the woman's face to see how she reacted to that statement. She smiled.

He knew she would keep his secret.

"Of course he could have had it by now himself if he had had the ambition to make a better bow and the courage to go hunting alone." Boso could not resist bragging to this adoring sister.

"Doesn't he ever hunt alone?" she asked.

"Not that I know of."

"Boy! You are brave, Brother! How will you resist bragging to him about your hunt alone?"

"Reckon I won't resist. Reckon I will give him a couple cockatoo feathers and tell him about the bird and the bush rat."

"Look, Boso," interrupted Nogo-Ma. "Look how your baby brother is jumping in my tummy. Must be he is anticipating this meat and mushroom meal as much as I am!"

"Honest?" Boso stared all agog at what a babe in the womb might realize.

"Honestly. Keep watching. You'll see him stretch his arms and legs and sometimes even try to do a somersault, it feels like."

Boso watched intently. "You think he knows when you are excited about something?"

"Yes, I think he senses my moods." The woman cradled her hands under her swollen abdomen. "I think he knows how much I want him."

"How do you know he is going to be a boy?"

"Oh, I am not positive, of course, but I just have this feeling. Woman's intuition, whatever. Besides, facts are on my side. Two out of three of your father's children are male."

"Really?"

"Truly. Stop and figure."

"Ama has one daughter and two sons. You're right there. Why do you suppose Ama doesn't have another baby? I've been grown big a long time now.'

"She did have one after she weaned you. Do you

remember?"

"No, I don't. What happened to it?"

"He died when he was born."

"Really? Do many babies die when they are born?" Why didn't he know? Why hadn't he paid attention before? Would his new baby brother die too?

"Quite a few die at birth, and many more die in the next few moons after birth. Over half the ones who live at birth die before they are old enough to have teeth."

"That's awful! What kills them?'

"Many die of the spirit-sickness (malaria). Spirits can enter through their soft spot before it closes, you know. That's why we don't name babies while they are so weak and vulnerable. We hope that if we don't call attention to them by naming them, the evil spirits won't notice them."

"I see", said the lad, eyeing the woman closely. His eyes fastened on her stomach now that she had invited him to look at her freely. "I hope this baby doesn't die." He felt a growing concern for this unborn half-brother. He had an interest in him now, a share in his well-being, since he had provided meat for the mother's sustenance.

"Me too! Oh, how I hope! I trust the baby cannot sense my fears."

"What fears?"

"I fear that something is wrong."

"What's wrong?"

"I don't know. But I have never been this sick and weak before while I was carrying my other children. Besides, I had the spirit-sickness for a whole moon a while back. My arms and legs are getting thinner and thinner. The women say the baby is finishing me."

"Oh, no!" Boso eyed her thin arms and legs. "He won't finish you off, will he?" He suddenly realized how much her friendship meant to him. She noticed things more than other women, it seemed. They talked of things he never discussed with anyone else.

"Do women die in childbirth?" Yes, he remembered

one who had. Uncle Kira's third wife had died many moons before, when she was giving birth to her first child. Oh, no, how frightening it must be to be a woman! They not only have evil spirits and stonemen to contend with, but they have childbirth and babies' soft spots as well!

"Some women do, but don't worry, Boso. This meat will do me good. It's the first time I've even felt hungry in a long time. Let's see if the cockatoo is done.

"Yes, it should be done first."

It was. Nogo-Ma served it in three portions on fresh banana leaves which Nogo had picked. She placed a helping of mushrooms and spinach with each portion of fowl and served it with a flourish to the boy first.

"To our great hunter!"

"Thanks."

For several minutes everyone was too busy eating to talk.

"Mm-mm, but this bird is good!"

"So are the mushrooms and spinach, Sis. I'm glad you found so many! There are enough to go with all the meat."

"And I am so glad we have meat," said the girl with a smile and shining eyes. "The only meat we have had since the last pig feast many, many moons ago, are the grasshoppers, shrimp and two rats I've been able to catch. Ama used to be pretty good at catching things, but she's too slow and weak now, even when she isn't sick."

"I'll have to see if I can't do better by you both, from now on, Sis. I never thought about you not having the kill from hunts without a boy in your home to shoot them for you. Tikira can hunt for Ama and I will hunt for you two.

Boso dropped his head guiltily as he thought of how few kills they shared with their own mother. More often than not, they ate their kill or their catch, all alone in their tapanda. If he was going to be a great man like his father he would evidently have to learn to consider women. Apa probably would hunt for his wives if he had the time. He was so busy protecting his wives and his tribe, and trying to win new land for their homes and gardens that he seldom had time to indulge in hunting.

"Do you suppose the tree kangaroo is done, Ama?" asked Nogo.

"It may be." Nogo-Ma lifted the burning embers and coals aside with her tongs. She brushed back the ashes and drew out the roasted animal.

After eating all they could hold, they lay back to chat, satisfied.

Boso noticed Nogo-Ma had fallen asleep, even though it wasn't yet dark

"I'd better be going back to the tapanda," he said, but instead he continued leaning against the woven pit-pit cane wall, chatting with his sister. His eyes were beginning to feel heavy when the distant yodel reached them. Wide awake instantly, Boso heard his grandfather answer from the nearby manhouse.

"*Patepape*," he said in farewell. "Here, Nogo. Give the tree kangaroo skin to your mother for the new baby," and he scuttled out the door with his bow and arrows.

CHAPTER TWO: HAUS KRAI (HOUSE CRY)

"What is it, *Kaisuwa*? What did they say?"

"Bad news."

"How bad?"

"People at Yago-Paita have seen three Kati-loma men coming home, crying the deathwail."

"Yago-Paita," thought Boso 'Where the cockatoo sleeps.' He had been there. He had gone with his father to Yago-Paita to exchange for bird-of-paradise feathers.

"Who yodeled the news?"

"Men from Yare heard it from men at Puri, and yodeled to let us know."

"Let's go meet them."

"It's almost dark."

"I'll gather pit-pit for a torch and we can take along a coal to light it with, as soon as it is too dark to see."

"Okay. I'll wrap the coal while you gather the pit-pit." Grandfather began to pluck some leaves in which to wrap the red hot coal.

The maita (crickets) began to sing as Boso returned with the pit-pit.

"Saa mbaa! Let's us two go!" said Boso. Just then his mother came over the hill from the direction of her garden, crying.

"I knew it! I knew it! What did I tell you, Father-of-my-sons? Don't tell me you have already gone to the spirit world!"

"We don't know yet, Daughter-in-law. Your husband, my son, may be one of the three clay-covered figures mourning their way home. Boso and I are going to meet them. Will you come too?"

"Come, Tikira. Come women. Let's go with them," she answered. "We will learn the terrible news sooner this way."

They met the wailing wounded trio at Sumbura Marketplace.

"How many are dead?" asked the old man.

"As far as we know, all but ourselves are dead," answered Naki-Pa.

"Ama, nana Apa-yo!" screamed Boso's mother, again and again. "Mother-oh-my-father-o! My husband is dead! Dead! Dead!"

Boso was crying with her.

"Is my father dead?" he demanded of Naki-Pa, not waiting for an invitation to speak. "Did you see him dead?" he asked loudly, above the women's wails.

"No, Boso, I didn't see him dead," said Naki-Pa with some hesitation.

"Then he may be alive!"

"No, my boy, he can't be alive. If you must know it all, he received such a vicious chop from an enemy's steel axe, that his shoulder and arm were severed from his body. Then he was swallowed up by the enemy on a high cliff. If there was any life left in him, they would have finished him off. When I saw them give him that terrible chop, and close ranks around him, I knew all was lost. I knew he was a goner and I feared I was too! I turned and fled, but I only received two more arrows in my back. One dropped out itself, and I pulled the other out as soon as I was out of their sight."

"Were they poisoned arrows, Naki-Pa? Will you die?'

"No, our attack took them completely by surprise. They had no time to put fresh poison on their weapons. With the witchdoctor's help I should be able to recover. I'm not so sure about Were-Pa and Sekere-Pa here."

"Your knee is wounded?" Kaisuwa asked Were-Pa.

"Yes, I got a pronged arrow in it in such a way that I could not get it out. And my leg gave way at the knee, every time I tried to step on it. Consequently, I fell by the wayside on this side of their village. I never even reached the thick of the battle. Naki-Pa picked me up and pulled the arrow out, on his retreat."

"And where is your wound?" Kaisuwa asked of Sekere-Pa.

"I got a spear in my shoulder and an arrow in my left kidney, from the back. They left me for dead, but our hero here revived me." Sekere-Pa paused, then screamed, "But I wish I were dead! My son, Sekere, lies dead back there on the battlefield, and he was too young to die! His first son is yet to be born! Sekere-yo-iyo-iyo!

Boso and the others joined in. "Yo-iyo-iyo!"

"Don't leave your Mother and Father, Sekere!"

"Yo-iyo-iyo-iyo."

"How shall I tell your Mother, Sekere-yo?"

"Iyo-iyo-iyo."

Sekere's father was too overcome with grief to continue. When he broke into sobs, Boso turned to *Naki-Pa* with tears streaming down his own cheeks and his voice also broken with sobs.

"Is my Uncle Kira d-d-dead? Did you see him dead?"

"Yes, *naki-si*, I did."

Boso's grandfather strangled his sobs long enough to ask, "Are you certain? How did he die?"

"His neck was broken. His head was nearly severed from his body by one of those new steel axes. The enemy had two of them. It was our first time to meet up with the *Kian'alinu's* (redman's) steel axes in battle. We have only heard of them until now."

"My sons! My sons-iyo!" wailed Kaisuwa.

"Yo-iyo-iyo-iyo!"

"Have you both left me for the spirit world in one day?"

"Yo-iyo-iyo-iyo."

They mourned non-stop to Kati-loma. Kaisuwa led the threnody part of the time. When he was unable to go on, Boso's mother sang the lead. When Boso wasn't joining the Yo-iyo chorus, he was sobbing, "Apa-yo! Nana Apa-yo!"

They stumbled with their wounded and their grief onto the porch of the tapanda manhouse without missing a beat in the threnody. Boso's kaisuwa built up the fire as more people joined them on the porch. Questions were asked and answers were repeated again and again as each new group joined the mourners. All five of Apa's wives lifted their voices together in the wail for their lost husband. Boso's mother, Apa's first wife, often led the wail. Uncle Kira's two wives mourned for their husband. Sekere's sole wife and mother cried for him. Soon the yard around the tapanda was filled with wailing widows, fatherless children, and friends of the fallen war heroes.

Boso succumbed to sleep, long after big-night (midnight), only to rouse again and again to add his sleepy, heartbroken wail to the sad chorus. The skies poured down teardrops like the eyes all around him.

"Oh, Apa! Apa-yo! My great Apa-yo! Have you left me before I could learn to understand how you are so great? Have you left me without teaching me how to be great like you? How can I learn without your example, without your instruction?"

Rain continued all the next morning until big-sun. Somehow among the milling mourners, Boso found himself next to Nogo-Ma. When she heard him cry those questions again she put an arm around his shoulders as people often do when they cry together, but the words she whispered in his ear were not a wail.

"Your father is not dead. I believe your father is alive."

"Nogo-Ma!" Boso stared at her in open-mouthed astonishment.

"Sh-sh. The rest wouldn't believe me. Go ahead and cry for your Uncle Kira, but save the tears for your father."

"How do you know?"

"I don't really know, of course. I just have this feeling. We'll just have to wait and see."

Hope sprang up in Boso's heart. "Apa-yo! Nana Apa-yo! Come to me! Come home to me!"

However when his Apa did not appear that day, nor the next, or the next, hope died again. Boso thought he had cried out all his tears but each morning when he woke again to the realization of all the deaths, his eyes overflowed again. "Apa! My Apa! Will I never see you again?"

Naki-Pa organized a posse among the men who came to mourn, and they went back to retrieve bodies, corpses. They searched and searched for Mambi's, but returned without it.

"Eaten, of course," they said. "He was the greatest warrior in sight of Mountain Giluwe. Of course they ate him to gain his strength and his magic."

Sekere's body was gone too. "Ah, yes, they ate him because he was so young and tender and full-fleshed." Boso shivered in the bright sun.

Apa's five wives came to the tapanda each day to cry. No woman in the whole tribe went to her garden. Work would have desecrated the memory of their men. The invincible warrior Mambi alone, must be mourned for a whole month without surcease, to give him the honor due him.

The dry clay covering Boso's body made him itchy. At least he had been careful not to get it in his eyes. Several had sore eyes from the irritation of the clay they had slapped on wildly in their grief. Kaisuwa and one or two women had cut off fingers at the first joint. Ama and one or two other wives had slit one or both of their earlobes, so that the blood trickled down their clay-covered shoulders and breasts.

The fourth morning Boso wakened to the realization that he might be crying for his empty stomach as much as for his father and uncle. He felt desperate. He might do something crazy if he didn't soon get something to eat, and get this clay off him right away! He managed to wait until the morning sun was hot, then he walked toward 'the bad place.' That was one habit still allowed in times of mourning. No one could stop the normal functions of the body. Once he had relieved himself out of sight of all eyes, he struck off for the Sugu River.

Boso scanned the water as he stripped off his bark belt, leaves, and net covering. How inviting it looked. He dived off the bank into a deep pool in the river. The clay softened and slipped from him, easing the itching instantly. Kicking his feet to keep afloat, he washed first his hands and then his face underwater. Oh, how good it felt to be rid of that plaster casing of clay! He flipped over to float on his back, scrubbing his body with his fingernails, and then rubbing more gently. As soon as he was completely free of clay, he swam to the shallows and waded, searching for shrimp. Fresh water shrimp was just what his starving tummy needed! He caught them with skillful hands and slipped them right into his mouth. They slid down easily and soon soothed the hunger pains. For the next two hours he alternated between delightful swims and shrimp hunts. The last dozen shrimp he encased in a leaf-pouch he quickly formed. He donned his belt, old leaves, and netting once again. He would have liked to search for new leaves to cover his backside, but that would give his secret away. He tucked the leaf-pouch into his belt. A few yards farther downstream he stepped into a pool of soft clay. He scooped up handfuls and rubbed them on his legs, stomach, back, arms and finally, gingerly, on his cheeks, forehead and hair. The sun would dry it before he reached the tapanda and maybe no one would know of his stolen comfort. He hoped they were crying too much to even notice his absenteeism.

He sat down on the outskirts of the crowd upon his return and only gradually worked his way into the center, crying as he went, and joining the yo-iyo chorus. When the darkness hid every move, he sidled over to sit by Nogo-Ma. She brushed her arm against his affectionately. He slipped the pouch from his belt into her open hand. As her fingers closed around it she reached over with her other hand and gave his a quick squeeze of thanks.

"For my baby brother," he whispered.

"Great son of my great husband," she murmured against his ear.

"Do you still think Apa's alive?"

"I don't know. I can't seem to feel anything anymore. But I do know I have never had a conscious feeling of his death."

The next day Nogo snuck Boso some sweet potatoes.

"Ama allowed me to dig them in the dark, lest she die of hunger before she can deliver this baby."

"Good, Sister. Dig her some every night. Apa would want her to eat, I know."

"Yes, that's true. But they wouldn't understand."

"No, they wouldn't. So you have to do it in the dark."

Boso survived another four days of clay-casing before he could endure it no longer again. At big-sun he slipped away with a piece of flint, and a piece of shale tucked into his wide bark belt. He longed to take his bow and arrows but he knew he didn't dare.

After a bath and a swim in the Sugu River, he came out on the opposite bank and headed for the deep bush toward Wakipanda. Once in the thick undergrowth he cut a good big spear and sharpened it almost needle-sharp with his cutting stones.

"Can I hope to get anything," he murmured softly, "when I am so weak with hunger? But Nogo-Ma and her baby need it so badly, I must try my hardest."

Searching for tracks of small game he found many mushrooms, which he ate raw with fresh rani, a crisp, crunchy green, that sprang up in beds like myrtle on the jungle floor. Oh, how good both tasted! When he had all the mushrooms and rani he cared for, he gathered a big bundle and wrapped it in leaves.

Finally he found signs of a trail used by several small animals. He camouflaged himself in the foliage and waited. At dusk he heard, and then made out the form of a large wallaby jumping his way. He raised his spear carefully but even the stealthy movement made the miniature kangaroo pause and twitch his nose in every direction. After some minutes he resumed his hops toward Boso.

The boy's timing was perfect. The spear pierced the heart of the knee-high creature even as it knocked it over. Boso could not resist one glorious whoop of victory! Immediately he berated himself. The evil spirits will hear you, fool, and come to eat you and your wallaby both!

He grabbed up his kill and his wrap of rani and mushrooms and ran as swiftly as he could through the jungle gloom and gathering darkness. Undergrowth snagged him and slashed him. Once he stumbled into prickly vines and cried aloud as he unwrapped them carefully from his feet, ankles and calves. Were evil spirits after him? Was a stoneman looking at him from the gloom? As soon as he was free of the vines he proceeded more carefully but with as much haste as possible. He finally emerged from the jungle and broke into a run. Up and down the hills and valleys and between the sweet potato gardens, he ran. He knew the path well. Over the vine bridge, up the hill to Lere, and then across the back way to Nogo-Ma's house. No one was there. They were still crying at the tapanda.

Boso found the tongs and dug out coals from the ashes which he blew until they flamed. By their light, he found everything he needed to get a good fire going. He went outside for more wood and when he had the fire big and hot, he found nogo-Ma's bamboo knives. He skinned and gutted the wallaby and put it to roast in the ashes, placing the burning embers over it.

He began a little threnody of his own as he unwrapped his rani and mushrooms.

"Oh, my Apa-yo-iyo. Forgive us for eating-yo-iyo." He stuffed mushrooms and rani into the shorter bamboos and added a little water, from the waist high water bamboo. "We love you, Apa-yo-iyo, but our stomachs are growling-yo-iyo-iyo. My baby brother might die-yo-iyo-iyo. Your son might die-yo-iyo-iyo, if I don't feed Nogo-Ma." Fortunately he found sweet potatoes left from Nogo's last-night digging. He peeled these with the bamboo knife and tucked them into the ashes around the wallaby. He went out and gathered more wood for the fire and added it to the dying blaze. He laid the bamboos against the wood.

Exhausted by grief, guilt, fears and the hunt, Boso lay down by the fire. His threnody soon sank to a murmur and finally to silence as he fell into a deep sleep.

He wakened to Nogo-Ma's voice.

"It's okay, Nogo. It's only our Boso, and if I'm not mistaken, he has cooked us some food!"

Boso sat up quickly and drew the unburned ends of wood to the center to blow them into flame.

"It must be nearly big-night!"

"Yes, Naki-Ma's tribe came to bring some gifts of shells in honor of our tribe's great losses, so we stayed later."

"They must have missed me, then."

"Yes, they did, but they weren't too critical. They know how young you are. They know how many days you have stayed right there and mourned, like a much older boy."

"Are you hungry?"

"You better believe we are! Especially at the smell of that meat!"

"I didn't know if Naki-Ma's tribe might have brought food. I have been crying to Apa to forgive us and I've prepared wallaby and mushrooms and rani."

"Oh, Boso, my, **son!** Truly you are like a son to me! Must be the Good Spirit is causing you to take the place of the sons which the evil spirits snatched from me."

"Ama-si," whispered Boso, calling her "Dear little mother" for the first time.

CHAPTER THREE: A SPIRIT? A GHOST?

Boso's mother's tribe brought gifts of cowry shells to honor the death of the great Mambi. They joined in the tears and the threnodies.

Tears wormed their way through the clay on Boso's cheeks as they had been doing now for fourteen days! Just when I think I have finished all my tears, they well up again like a spring in me, he thought.

He and Tikira were standing before their mother's people. The women were caressing them, mulling them, almost as they would have done to Mambi's corpse if it had been there.

"How can you two become warriors-iyo-iyo-iyo?

"When your father is now dead-iyo-iyo-iyo?

"A great man! He could have trained you!-iyo-iyo-iyo.

"To be great like himself-iyo-iyo-iyo.

"But now you are fatherless-iyo-iyo-iyo.

"*Naana kale-naki lapo*yo-iyo-iyo-iyo. Our two orphan boys-iyo-iyo-iyo."

There was a lull in the wailing long enough for keen ears to pick up a distant yodel.

"Yo-iyo?"

Koiyamu, Naki's older cousin, ran to the knob behind the *tapanda* and yodeled back.

"Yes-iyo-iyo?"

"There's an evil spirit coming toward my garden-iyo."

"An evil spirit, you say-iyo?"

"An evil spirit or some sort of creature. It walks on legs like a man sometimes, then it goes on its belly like a snake sometimes-iyo."

"Who's calling?"

"I'm Su-Ma, working in my garden. The creature is coming from Sakamapi-way."

"You still see it?"

"I still see it, but I cannot make out if it is a man, an animal, or an evil spirit."

"We will come to guard you. Keep your eye on it-iyo."

Koiyamu returned to the crowd. "Who will go with me?"

"I will," responded Boso.

"Me too. Me too," echoed Tikira and Naki.

Boso's mother's youngest brother stepped forward. "I'll accompany you boys," he said fingering the stone axe tucked into his bark belt. "You'd better have a man along."

They headed up the hill on the run while the threnody resumed its sad wail behind them.

"Who is this Su-Ma, besides being the mother of a boy named Su?" asked Uncle.

"She belongs to a tribe from Warea who are friendly to us," answered the boys. Koiyamu was leading but Boso soon came abreast of him where the path widened.

"Let's keep together, Boso, in case it is an evil spirit, or a wounded animal or man."

"Maybe it's a crazy man," suggested Boso.

"Possibly."

They reached Su-Ma's garden. The woman pointed at

a far hillside across a deep ravine.

"Watch in the kunai grass just above that highest sweet potato garden and you'll see it in a bit. It came out of that patch of trees on the crest there."

"Can you see it, boys?" asked Koiyamu. He had lost one eye in a mock battle when the men were teaching the boys how to fight. He hadn't lifted his shield in time and another boy's arrow had got him in the eye. It appeared that his remaining eye wasn't as strong as it should be either.

"I see it," said Boso's Uncle. "Look, boys, just to the left of that goroka-nut tree."

"Yes. Something's moving there," agreed Boso.

"You keep your eye on it and on us, Su-Ma," said Uncle, "and we'll go down and cross that stream and start up toward it. If at any time you can make out better what it is, call to us."

"Will do."

Uncle led the way this time, with Boso right behind him. They descended to the stream, crossed it and started up the other side. When they emerged from the thick woods growing along the stream and came about level with Su-Ma's garden, Uncle yodeled back to her.

"Su-Ma-yo."

"Yo."

"Do you see us-iyo?"

"I see you-iyo."

"Do you see it-iyo?"

"I see it. It is almost to the garden, now, but it hasn't moved for a little bit."

They resumed their climb. Ahead there was another dip. Descending it, they were out of sight of Su-Ma again for a while. When she saw them again she called to them.

"I see you. It still hasn't moved-iyo."

Through one garden on a gradual slope, through a big patch of pitpit cane into a second garden, the man and boys walked single file between the sweet potato mounds.

"One more field of kunai grass and we should reach that garden."

"Yes, Uncle," responded Boso and Tikira.

Boso soon found he was shaking badly. His knees felt weak. Would they see a real evil spirit? He turned around to see the other three boys hanging back.

"Come on, you kids!" He tried to command roughly in the sternest voice he could muster.

They caught up to him slowly. Mentally he sternly commanded his own knees not to shake. He quickened his step behind his Uncle.

When they reached the top edge of the kunai field they crouched and studied the garden and the kunai grass beyond it and above it. For a while they saw nothing. Just when they were beginning to breathe normally there was a fearful thrashing in the grass.

Boso's liver seemed to force its way upward and clog his breathing passage. He dropped on all fours as he fought for air. The thrashing ceased and his liver slipped down again.

"What could it be?" murmured Uncle.

No one offered an answer. Maybe no one else could talk.

"Well, let's go closer."

Again no one responded.

Uncle turned to look at the boys. "Anyone brave enough to come with me?"

"I am," croaked Boso, in a voice he could hardly recognize as his own.

"*Saa mbaa*, Nephew. Let's us two go." He reached for Boso's hand. "It will be better if there are two of us."

Boso felt a surge of courage as his Uncle's hand grasped his. He stood upright and they started into the garden. They were halfway across it when the thrashing resumed. Boso sank to his knees while Uncle scrutinized the grass. Boso likewise never took his eyes from the spot. A low moaning reached their ears.

"Something wounded. Man or animal?" murmured the man.

"I can't tell, Uncle."

"Neither can I. The death cries of some animals sound almost human. At any rate, I don't think it can hurt us."

"Would evil spirits ever act like that to trick people into coming close enough to grab them?" Boso forced the question through stiff lips in a squeaky voice.

"I never heard of it."

"Or stonemen?"

"Stonemen stand still and stare at you. They know their looks can kill. They don't need to employ any tricks."

Uncle's words helped Boso rise to his feet. Hands clasped, they inched their way slowly forward, ready to turn and run if necessary. There was no more thrashing. They reached the edge of the garden.

"I think it's a man." Uncle was taller and could see better into the high grass.

"Yes, it's a man."

Uncle pulled Boso forward and they stood at the side of a man lying face downward in the grass.

"Look at those vines bound around his body and one shoulder. He must be badly wounded.

A scream tore out of Boso's throat! "Could it be Apa?"

"Quickly but gently, they rolled the man over on his back.

"It is, isn't it? Or isn't it?" the face was so thin and bony! The body so shrunken! The eyes so sunken!

"See here, Boso. The shoulder's been badly chopped, nearly severed from his body. It must be Mambi! It has to be Mambi!"

"Apa! Apa-yo! Apa! Apa-yo!" screamed Boso.

The sunken eyes fluttered open briefly.

"Boso," came the feeble whisper. The dehydrated lips tried to smile.

Boys came running through the garden to them, at sound of Boso's screams.

"Quick, boys, help me fix a stretcher!"

They cut two poles, gathered vines and kunai grass. While Uncle bound the poles together with vine, Boso furiously wove the kunai grass for the bed. The boys kept him supplied with grass. Uncle helped him weave one side over one pole and fasten it With more grass and vine they quickly fastened the other side.

Koiyamu helped Uncle lift Mambi onto the stretcher. Mambi groaned in pain and opened his eyes again.

Boso grabbed his hand. "It's all right, Apa. We'll carry you the rest of the way home."

"*Ipa*," whispered Mambi. "*Ipa!*"

"Of course, Apa. You want water. You're dying of thirst. We'll get you water in a jiffy."

The three boys helped lift the stretcher to Koiyamu's and Uncle's shoulders as gently as possible. Boso hung on to his father's hand. Tikira raced ahead.

"Su-Ma-iyo-iyo!"

"Yo?"

"Tell them it's Apa. Yodel and tell them we are bringing Apa home."

They lowered the stretcher by the stream while Tikira was forming a leaf cup. They held the filled cup to Mambi's lips and he gulped it frantically.

"More! More!"

Boso lost count of how many cupfuls his father drank. At last he said, "*Manda*," and sank back. "Enough," and he slumped into sleep or unconsciousness. Boso didn't know which.

They raised the stretcher to their shoulders again and started the ascent. Before they reached Su-Ma's garden, people were swarming them.

"Is it Mambi?"

"Is it really Mambi?"

"Will he live?"

"Is he unconscious?"

"Is it our bigman? Really? Truly?"

"Make way! Make way!" yelled Uncle. "Let us get Mambi through! It is Mambi himself! The invincible warrior Mambi still isn't dead! If we take care of him right he may live to fight again!"

For the Katiloma tapanda and women's house mourning came to a standstill. They could cry for the other men later. They had received their Big-Man (chief) back from the dead, as it were, and they must fight to help him live!

Boso gleefully ran out to do the first chore assigned him.

"Help me catch a piglet, and we will kill it and offer it to the spirits and to your father," commanded his Kaisuwa.

Boso and Tikira accompanied Grandfather to the area where their mother's biggest sow had farrowed two months earlier. While the other two distracted the sow with scrap sweet potatoes, Boso snagged one of the piglets and then ran for his life, to escape the angry sow.

While Kaisuwa was dressing the piglet and worshipping the spirits ceremonially, Boso went to help his mother gather garden greens to cook in the blood they had caught in a bamboo after slitting the piglet's throat. He had asked Kaisuwa to let him watch the ceremony to the spirits, but grandfather had sent him away saying, "Even Tikira isn't old enough for that yet. Go play! Enjoy your childhood! It is risky enough trying to appease the evil spirits when you are a mature man!"

"The witchdoctors are already working on Apa," he said to Ama as they gathered the delicious komba greens with purple hearts at the center of every leaf. "They say his shoulder has already begun to knit back to his body. They say it is such a fine job of splinting that they wonder if he found a friend to help him. They cannot believe he could have done that himself in his condition."

"Don't they realize your father can do anything? Don't they know by now that he is magic? That he's powerful?

That he's indestructible? If they didn't know it last moon they should know it now! Who else could survive alone in the bush with such a wound? Who else could have escaped his enemies like that, after they had 'closed ranks' around him, as reported? Tell those witchdoctors, 'Of course, he bound up his own shoulder! If he'd have found a friend, that friend would have brought him home or got word to us long before this!'"

"You're right, Ama. That's what Kaisuwa said."

"By the way, where is my sister? She should be helping us get this food ready for Apa."

"She's gone back home to tell her new husband the news of her father's magical return. She said she will come back to see him again tomorrow."

Boso was present when Grandfather presented the food to Apa. "May I present pork, and blood-soaked *komba*, to our Big-Man who has returned to us from the spirit-world, as it were? Rise and eat, my son!"

Mambi drank some broth first, and later he even ate a little pork, and a good helping of the purplish komba boiled in blood and water. Boso was given a tiny portion of the pork and *komba* along with all the sweet potatoes he could eat. How delicious! But his conscience pricked him as he ate the pork. He should have been saving it to give to Nogo-Ma. On the other hand, he knew women were not allowed to eat such food, that had been offered to the spirits. Only males. He promised himself he would go hunting for bush-marsupials for her the next day if his father didn't need him.

Mambi healed faster than anyone supposed possible. The very next morning he crawled out of the tapanda to sit in the sun. Soon he fell fast asleep on his *pandanus* (goroka-nut) umbrella mat, absorbing the sun's healing rays. Boso sat beside him awhile, thrilling to the look of health already returning to his father's face. The eyes weren't so sunken. The cheeks and lips weren't so dehydrated and emaciated. This man was looking more like his beloved father already.

He could have whooped for joy, but instead he sat very quietly, unwilling to disturb his father's healing sleep. Finally he arose and slipped back into the manhouse to get his father's drinking gourd, and his bows and arrows. He laid the gourd within reach of his father's hand.

"You'll get well, my Apa," he told himself in his mind. "You'll get well and you will teach me how you came to be such a great man. You'll instruct me in courage, in self-control, and even in gentleness and care for women and children. You'll teach me how to survive in situations where anyone else would die. You'll teach me how to be invincible and indestructible like yourself."

Boso hurried to the bush. When he handed the two parrots to Nogo-Ma that afternoon he said, "I'm off to see Apa. I can't wait to get back to him."

"Will you come to help us eat the two birds when they are cooked?"

"Maybe. If you save a leg for me, I will come over after dark, if Apa is asleep."

She handed him his favorite type of sweet potato.

"Thank you, Ama-si."

"Thank you, my son, for the parrots. Isn't it wonderful to have your father home?"

"Wonderful! Marvelous! Terrific! Super-out-of-this-world wonderful! You were right, Ama-si. You were right all along. Apa was alive. Apa didn't die. What a smart woman you are!"

"Not smart. Just intuitive. Your father is the love of my life. I felt sure my heart would tell me if he died."

Back at the manhouse, Apa was awake and they were pestering him with questions. Boso was immediately hot with temper. Why didn't they have enough sense to leave his poor father alone? If they had been boys he would have taken a piece of firewood and bashed this way and that until he had routed everyone but Apa. But they were not boys. They were men. He didn't dare even speak, disrespectfully. Instead he sat down by his father, though he was seething.'

"How did you get away from them when they had closed ranks around you like that?" they asked again and again. Apa only sat there with his eyes closed, and a little half-smile on his lips. After the tenth question he opened his eyes, and said softly, even gently, "Later, my friends, I will tell you all later."

Some men had the sense to look sheepish. No one broke the gentle silence.

"After tomorrow, when I have eaten more pork, and had two days to digest it and grow stronger, I'll tell you all my story."

The anger in Boso's heart melted away at his father's gentle words. How long would it take him, he wondered, to learn to treat exasperating people with gentleness.

Boso settled himself beside Tikira in the very front when the crowd gathered to hear Mambi's story. Why shouldn't they have the best seats? After all, they were his *sons!*

Naki-Pa has told you about the vicious chop I received to my left shoulder, and then how the enemy closed around me. I had not time to look at my wound. I only knew that my left arm could no longer hold my shield. I managed to grab at it with my right hand before my left hand dropped it. So I was holding both my stone axe and my shield with my right hand. I could no longer fight the enemy. I could only shield my wound from their eyes. When they closed in between me ·and my men, I began backing away from them. I didn't dare turn or I would have received an arrow, or a spear, or an axe in my back. Besides, they would have seen my wound from the back view and been on me instantly like a herd of wild boar.

"Consequently, I kept backing away from them, trying to lengthen the distance between us. They kept coming, but not as fast as I was retreating. Suddenly I knew from the gleam in their eyes that all was not right behind me. I turned enough to see that I was only two footsteps away from the edge of a ledge. Two more backward steps and I would doubtless have fallen to my death."

Mambi paused and looked at his sons. "Always remember to watch your enemies' body language or signs, my sons. Often their expressions and movements tell you more than their words.

'There was no escape through that line of warriors, and no other escape route."

Boso became aware that he was holding his breath.

"I had to jump."

Boso heard the listeners gasp in unison.

"So jump I did! I threw my axe first and then, still gripping my shield well away from my body, I gave a fearful leap right over the treetops below me!

"I landed in clay.

Boso heard the audience sigh out the breath they had gasped in.

"I sunk to my knees in the yellow clay.

"Stuck there, as though I was rooted to the spot, I had time to look at my wound. When I saw that my left arm was nearly severed from my body, I said to myself, 'Old Boy, you may be finished this time.' But I decided not to give up just yet.

"You know what we are going to have to do, Brothers and Sons?"

"What?"

"We're going to have to get ourselves some steel axes. We will have to stop fighting for awhile anyway. We must arrange a trading mission."

"What can we offer for trade?"

"Feathers. Flint. I don't know what all. We'll think about that later.

"Well, as I was saying, I said to myself, 'Old Boy, you may be finished this time. You've got to get out of here in a hurry or you will be finished.' I extricated myself from the clay, one leg at a time. Then I picked up my shield again and located my axe. Finally I had time to look around and notice my location and assess my next move.

"Guess what I saw ahead."

"A river?"

"*Ndia* (No)."

"Another cliff?"

"*Ndia*."

"More of the enemy?"

"Right. A whole village which I figured housed more of the enemy."

"A whole village?"

"A whole village. But I didn't have time to stand there and gaze and ponder for long. I could hear, 'Kati! Kati!' war whoops from men finding an alternate route down that cliff. I knew they might soon be upon me.

"So I grasped my shield in my right hand again. I held the shield low enough to show my face, but high enough to hide my wound. I screamed the loudest, most blood-curdling 'Kati!' I've ever managed and I charged that village."

Boso gasped again as the superb storyteller paused for effect.

"What happened?" asked Tikira.

"People came scrabbling out of their houses and scurrying in all directions. None of them came at me, however. Old men, women, children, young boys, sick people. I guess they thought I was a whole tribe coming to burn down their houses, and they'd better escape to the bush.

"I didn't turn aside to chase anyone, of course. I ran straight on through, as fast as I could go, and I kept running until I was in deep bush, and was absolutely positive no one was following me.

"Then I stopped long enough to find the best kind of vine-rope for tying my arm to my body. I took time and tried to do a perfect job so I wouldn't have to ever redo it. As soon as I had completed that, I found water. I had a long ways to go to find it because I seemed to have stuck to the ridge, but I was desperate for a drink to help replace all the blood I'd lost, so everything else became secondary. I located a stream. After I had drunk my fill I followed the stream up to a place where I found wild bananas and a bush garden. I holed up there near that water for three days, giving my enemy long enough to be sure I was dead, and giving myself a chance to get over the worst of my soreness.

"The next morning I crossed under cover of the jungle to the ridge on the other side of the valley and began working my way home. It was slow going. In my wounded condition it was imperative that I keep hidden from all enemies so I went in circuitous routes around all villages. Many times I went too long without water or food and became nearly crazed with thirst. But I made it. I made it almost home. Given another night, I'd have come crawling in here to my own *tapanda*. Truly though, it was nice to relax on that stretcher and let you carry me to water, fill me full, then carry me home!

"Water is the sweetest thing to a dying man. Remember that, boys," he said, looking at his sons. "Always take water to the wounded when you go to fetch your comrades home.

"But now, sweeter even than water to the wounded, is the chance to be home with my own people, alive and getting well. Life is good, my Sons, my Brothers. Thank the Good Spirit for life. We thank him for a pink cowry shell, or a red pig, or a son or especially a light-skinned baby boy. But thank him for life ~ the best gift!

CHAPTER FOUR: BIRD LANDING STRIP

"Yo-iyo! Yo-iyo-iyo-iyo!" The yodeling call came from over the mountains. "Calling all men and boys-yo-iyo!"

"Yo?"

"The white man's police-boys have come to recruit workers for the Kagua airstrip. All men and boys are required to appear for directions."

Boso and Tikira went to Mambore with their father and grandfather and other men from the surrounding tribes and villages.

The policemen chose the older boys and men who they felt were able to work.

"What happened to your shoulder?"

Mambi told his story.

"You rest and heal for two more moons and then you can come to work too."

"*Manda.*"

A policeman put his hand on Tikira's shoulder. "This boy is big enough to work." Pointing at Boso he continued, "This one isn't."

"What is an airstrip?" the men inquired of one another.

"It's where those big birds come and land. You know those great big birds that fly over, making all that noise and carrying all that cargo from the spirit world to our world? We'll get rich after we make a landing place for those big birds," answered some men from east of Mambore, men who evidently knew what they were talking about. "Those birds will bring us steel axes, red cloth, beads, cowry shells and fish in *tsin* cans ~ straight from our departed ancestors, but it takes a white man to know how to call the birds in."

Boso listened to the men discuss the bird news on the way home.

"How many days do you suppose a man will have to work to earn a steel axe?"

"No idea."

"I'd work many moons for one," said Mambi. "I know how they can cut!"

"Pretty sharp, are they?"

"You better believe it! Why, I imagine one of them would cut firewood as easily as a bamboo knife cuts through pig grease. That enemy's axe cut my flesh and bone just that easily."

The man he was talking to clicked his thumb nail off his two front teeth.

"We won't have to try to find someone to trade or barter with as we had thought. We can go trade work for the white man's goods," continued Mambi. "I've been clearing ground for my fifth wife's gardens to try to gain strength in this shoulder and arm the last several days. But now I'll go at it more vigorously and try to keep at it longer so I can gain strength to work in Kagua."

"I wish I could grow big faster so I could go work," exclaimed Boso.

"Enjoy your carefree days, my Son. Hunt and fish and swim and play. You'll be a man loaded down with responsibilities soon enough.

Boso headed for his mother's gardens as soon as he got home.

"Ama, I'm starving. What can I have to eat?"

There are some cooked sweet potatoes in my *bilum* (net-bag), hanging on that palm tree there," she pointed with her nose as she went on digging with her stick.

"Good. I thought I was going to die on the road."

Boso got the sweet potatoes and sat down by his mother to tell her the news of the bird-landing strip while he ate.

"I've got news too," said Ama at last.

"What's that?"

"Nogo-Ma went to the bush to have her baby this morning."

"Really?"

"Really."

"How soon can I go see my baby brother, after he's born?"

"Not until she returns to the village. Bush huts are strictly out of bounds for boys. You know that!"

"How long will she stay in the bush?"

"Oh, one moon or so, give or take a few days either way."

"That's a long time to wait to see the baby."

"You need to learn patience, my son."

Boso went to all of Nogo-Ma's gardens the next day, looking for Nogo. His search was finally rewarded.

"You're digging sweet potatoes," he called to his sister in greeting as he approached her.

"Yes, guess what?"

"What is it? A boy or a girl?"

"You have a new baby brother."

"Ama-si was right then. When was he born?" "Early this morning.

"Is he well and strong?"

"Yes. He's a very nice baby."

"Wish I could see him!"

40

"I wish you could too!"

"How's your mother?"

"Not very good."

"Is she eating?"

"A little. She's very weak. Weaker than I've ever seen her before."

"Is she nursing the baby all right?"

"Oh, yes. He's a strong baby. He's nursing very well."

"I wish I had some meat to give you for her. If I can get some, how could I get it to her?"

"I could meet you here at this same time tomorrow."

"Manda. We'll plan that."

Boso had two *giligalas* for Nogo when they met the next day. "Sorry I couldn't get anything bigger," he apologized.

"These are fine. They will be delicious cooked with greens. Ama will be able to eat them, I'm sure. I caught some crickets for her this morning and she ate them, but these *giligalas* (miniature parrot) will be so much tastier."

Three days later Mambi trapped a cassowary. His wives and father and the other men and boys, not strong enough or old enough to work in Kagua, helped him prepare a mumu to cook the huge ostrich-like bird. Boso carried firewood and more firewood to heat the stones red hot, while Ama and the other women peeled green bananas and sweet potatoes with their bamboo knives.

Hours later when they removed the steaming hot food from the pit in the ground Boso snitched some too soon and burned his fingers.

"Apa, this is delicious!" he said around the fingers he was sucking both to cool them and savor every bit of the taste.

"Could I take a portion of bananas and greens and cassowary to Nogo-Ma, Apa? She's not doing very well since the baby was born."

"Certainly."

Boso carried the food wrapped in banana leaves into the bush in the right direction and then yodeled for Nogo.

"Yo? I'm coming." It didn't take her long, so the birth hut could not be too far away.

"Guess what I have for your mother?"

"Do you have some of that cassowary they say Apa trapped?"

"Exactly!"

"Oh, won't she love that!"

"How's the baby doing?"

"He's stronger than ever. He nurses all the time, it seems, and cries very loudly sometimes. Ama thinks he's the strongest son she has ever had. She says he will grow to be like you. She thinks he even looks like you."

"Really? Do you think so?"

"I don't know. I can't tell. He's a good-looking baby though."

"Well, tell her to eat cassowary and get strong so she can come home soon. I want to see this baby that looks like me."

* * * *

Boso was working with Apa, clearing ground several days later when they heard a girlish yodel.

"Apa-yo. Apa-yo-iyo!"

"Yo –Nogo-yo. I'm here."

"Apa-yo. Ama komaande. Ama komaande."

Boso's heart stood still. Nogo-Ma was dead! No! Surely not! Oh, surely that couldn't be true! He took off on a run to the bush trail.

Disregarding everything he had been told he ran right to the hut. He could hear Nogo crying and calling her mother. He crawled inside. As soon as his eyes adjusted somewhat to the darkness he crawled over to Nogo-Ma. He put his hand on her arm, then over her nose and mouth. Yes, her spirit and breath had left her. And here was the baby snuggled in the circle of her left arm. He picked up the baby, bilum and all.

Oh, yes! He was a nice baby. Look at all that black hair!

Boso touched the soft curls with one finger. He wished his own hair felt that soft. He rubbed his hand over the little head, petting him. What a handsome baby boy! What would a baby do without a mother? Suddenly realization flashed on him, shocking him. They always buried tiny babies with their mothers! But he couldn't let them bury his baby brother, could he? Oh, no! He must save him! He must do his best to save him.

He looked wildly around the hut. It was filling fast with women. They didn't seem to be noticing him however. He slipped the bilum ends up into each hand, draping the baby between them. He lifted it around one shoulder to his back and tied the two ends at his chest level in front. He sighed a big sigh of relief. Now he had the baby safely. No one could take him from him.

The women were cyring, screaming, wailing. He could hear Nogo's voice above the others. "Ama! Ama-yo! Please don't leave me! Please don't leave me!"

Boso relaxed a little more and listened to the wailing. Tears were sliding down his own cheeks at the thought of never hearing another word from his little Ama-si, never receiving another inquiring look from her kind, intelligent eyes.

"But I'll help, Amasi," he murmured aloud through his tears. "I'll help your dream come true. I'll try to help keep this baby alive so he can grow up to be brave and strong like Apa, and wonderful and special like you. Oh, my Ama-si!"

"Ama-yo! Ama, come back to me!" cried Nogo.

"We better carry her body outside. The men are here with the bark, ready to put her in," said one of Boso's aunts.

The women lifted the corpse and managed to get it out through the small door of the unclean hut. They had to manage it themselves because men didn't dare enter. Boso exited with them. The women lowered the body into the open-ended canoe-like bark wrapping which Mambi and his friends had prepared. Once the body was completely encased in the bark, the men took over.

"Where's the baby?" asked one.

Boso tightened his grip on the *bilum* ends. A woman crawled back through the low door.

"He's not in here," she called out.

Boso saw Nogo's tear-filled eyes on him.

"Boso has him," she said softly through her tears.

"Give him to us, Boso, so we can tie him into the bark with his mother."

"No. No. I want to carry him."

"Oh, all right," agreed Apa. "Let him carry him to the village. We can easily slip him into the bark there."

They tied supple vines around the bark, closing it into a cocoon, and made a loop of vine above the closure at each end. They slipped a pole into these loops and hoisted the bark cocoon to their shoulders.

The men went first with the body. The women followed behind, crying their threnody, keening their death wail.

"My friend, oh, my friend-iyo. You were such a good woman-iyo –iyo –iyo-iyo.

"You made so many gardens, iyo –iyo –iyo.

"You harvested so many sweet potatoes, *taro*, sugar cane and *komba*-yo –iyo –iyo –iyo.

"You bore so many sons –iyo –iyo –iyo.

"Now you've followed these sons to the spirit world – iyo –iyo-iyo.

"Why did you have to go-iyo –iyo-iyo?

"Why did you have to hear them calling-iyo –iyo –iyo?

"Why did you respond-iyo –iyo –iyo?

"Oh, my friend, my dear little sister, come back! Come back, I beg you –iyo –iyo –iyo!"

Oh, if only she could come back, thought Boso. How on earth am I going to keep this baby alive? Will I be able to find a woman to nurse him? Do I dare ask a woman? That might not be a proper question. Maybe I can get Ama to ask.

The men put the pole on two forked sticks stuck into the ground on the *singsing* oval. The women swarmed around Ama-si's body and cried. Some of them caressed her hair with their fingers. Others pawed her feet as they wailed.

The men sat in the shade of the huge spreading bamboo and talked quietly among themselves. Boso walked around the women, stood among them crying, pulling on the ends of the baby's bilum, sliding his hands down them, pawing them as the women were doing the the hair and feet of Nogo-Ma. Boso stood near Nogo and joined her sad chorus. Slowly he became aware that he was the only boy crying, the only boy mingling among the wailing women, the only boy joining in the threnody. But he felt safer here. If he went and sat down with the men, they might try to take his baby from him. It was best to stay right here and cry.

Storm clouds were moving in and Boso realized it was mid-afternoon. Distant thunder rumbled. Several men got to their feet and moved toward the women.

"It's time to put the corpse into the ground," said one. "We must be dispersing before the rain."

Two men lifted the pole from the forked sticks, placed it on their shoulders and carried it to the shallow grave some older boys had dug. There they lowered the pole with its bark cocoon to the ground, and slipped the pole from the vine loops.

"Boso! Boso-yo," called one of the men.

"Where is that boy?" said another.

Boso purposely hovered on the outskirts of the crowd, as far from the grave as possible.

"Boso! Bring the baby!"

A boy pushed Boso forward.

Boso's knees felt like lard left too close to the fire. He wanted to sit down, but he dare not. Put a stone into your liver and fight this through, he said to himself, but could he buck the whole tribe? How could one little boy stand against all those adults?

He squared his small bony shoulders and faced the men.

"NO! I am not going to give you the baby. I am going to keep him!"

"You can't keep him, Boy! He'll die," said one.

"Where is your milk? Show us your breasts," taunted another. "How will you nurse him?"

"Don't be foolish, Boso," said a kinder voice. "There is no way you can keep a baby alive without his mother. You will have to bury him in the end, so you might as well bury him now."

"No! I won't bury him now! If he dies, I will bury him then. But I'm not burying him alive."

'I'm not digging another grave," said a boy.

"You won't have to," screamed Boso. "I'll dig his grave myself if he dies!"

"Boso, you're not being reasonable." The man started toward Boso, reaching out his hand.

Boso spun on one heel and darted out of the crowd. With one hand he held the *bilum* knot at his chest. His other hand grasped the *bilum* at his back, pressing it against himself, lest he bounce the baby too much as he ran. He gained a small knoll and realized he did not hear any footsteps following him.

He turned around and viewed the crowd from his vantage point. No. No one had followed him far. No one had actually chased him. They were going to let him keep his baby. He let his knees fold under him and he sat. But he watched their every movement, ready to rise and run if one should come in his direction. They talked for a while, evidently undecided. Thunder rumbled again and two men immediately stooped down and lifted the bark cocoon. They placed it gently in the grave and laid banana leaves over it, wrapping them partially around it. Then they stepped back and began pushing loose dirt into the grave with their bare feet. Other boys and men came forward to help.

Boso sighed a sigh so deep it seemed to come from the soles of his feet.

"You're mine, little Brother. You're all mine now," he said aloud.

Rain drops started falling. The men and boys worked faster, tamping the dirt down underfoot. Boso turned and began walking quickly in the direction of the *tapanda*. Boys sped by him and were already seated by the fireplace when he got there. Men arrived at the same time.

"Well, you've got yourself a baby."

"You'll find a baby harder to feed than a pet possum or piglet."

"You don't know what you have let yourself in for."

Boso tried to shut his ears, but no, he must not do that. He must listen for his father's voice. What would Apa say? Why didn't Apa say something? Boso sat with lowered head, digging his bare toes into the ashes of the fireplace while everyone but Apa voiced their opinions. All negative. Nobody thought he had done the right thing.

Finally Boso began darting furtive glances this way and that to ascertain where Apa had seated himself. When he located him among some men from Nogo-Ma's tribe he stood to his feet and wriggled between the seated forms until he reached Apa. He knelt in front of him and brought the *bilum* around and opened it, almost in Apa's lap.

"Look, Apa. He's a nice boy."

Apa sat silently looking at his newest son. Boso couldn't tell how he felt by looking at his face. Wasn't he going to say anything? At length, he spoke.

"Yes. Son. He's a nice boy."

"I couldn't let them bury him alive, Apa."

"He will die, son."

"But he has to have a chance, Apa. It's not fair to smother him with dirt. Why! We wouldn't do that to a pig! Why should we do it to my baby brother? To your son?"

"It would be quicker than watching him starve to death, son."

A sob tore at Boso's throat. He could hardly speak. He forced himself to get the words past the lump in his throat, and they came out louder than he meant for them to, in the quiet *tapanda*.

"He won't starve! I won't let him starve! I'll do something!"

Boso stood up, trembling, and shakily tied the *bilum* around his shoulders. He wormed his way through the men and boys to his umbrella. Slipping it over his head and baby and *bilum*, he started out in the rain to his mother's hut. He couldn't stay there with all that disapproval any longer.

"I'm coming, Ama," he said as he crouched to enter the low doorway.

"Come, my boy."

"I've brought the baby to show you." Boso untied the *bilum* and laid back the ends once again. "Isn't he a nice boy?"

"Yes, he is. He looks a lot like you did when you were that size."

"That's what Nogo's mother said."

"His face is a little broader than yours, but you both look like your father."

"I couldn't let them bury him alive."

"No, my son. Being you, you couldn't."

"What do you mean?"

"When you were a toddler, I gave you a piglet of your own. You wrapped your arms around it, and said, 'Mine! Mine!' You wouldn't let anyone else touch it. We nicknamed you, Kanga, Grubworm, because your arms were turned in on yourself like the two ends of a grubworm. Now here you are doing the same thing to this baby."

"But this is different, Ama."

"How is it different?"

"Oh, I don't know. How shall we two feed him, Ama.
Ama smiled at the 'we two.'

"Did you have anything in mind?"

"Well, I thought maybe we could… maybe you could ask some woman to share her baby's milk with our baby."

"No, Boso, we can't do that."

"Why not?"

"All of us women have more children than we can provide for already. We grow old and skinny bearing our husband's children and trying to raise enough gardens to feed them. When we work too hard we age too fast, and then our husband has to buy a younger, fatter wife to please him. You can't ask that of any woman."

"But he's such a nice baby."

"No matter"

"Well, what can we do then? We can't just watch him starve to death."

"No. You'll have to chew sugar cane, and spit the juice into his mouth. That's the only thing I know to do."

"Can I get some sugar cane from your garden, Ama?"

"Yes."

"Right now?"

"Right now, before he starts crying."

"He was crying a while ago at the *singing* ground, but he went back to sleep."

"You had better hurry then. Leave him here. Don't take him out into the rain when you don't have to. He's too young to be out of the house at all."

Boso dashed out and was back before his mother could have believed possible, with two long sticks of sugar cane. One yellow and one red. His baby was wriggling and whimpering.

Boso quickly broke off a third of one stick and began peeling it with his strong white teeth. He took a bite and chewed it, but when he started to remove the pulp from his mouth he automatically swallowed the juice.

"Whoops, I swallowed that mouthful." He tried again.

This time he managed to keep the juice in his mouth while he extracted the pulp with his fingers. He held the baby, *bilum*, mat, and all on his knees. He touched his own lips against the baby's lips, and baby immediately opened his mouth. Boso let him have half of his mouthful of cane juice, but it was too much. Baby gasped like he was drowning, and let most of it run out of his mouth while he squirmed and wriggled and fought to breathe. As soon as he got his breath again, he made sucking motions with his mouth, savoring the sweet taste.

"Just a little at a time, Boso. Just a very little."

Boso lowered his lips again and gave a small squirt between his teeth. It was just right. Baby sucked contentedly. But in no time he found he was only sucking his own tongue. The sweet taste was all gone. He gave a sharp cry of frustration. Again Boso lowered his lips to give him another squirt, but just then baby turned his lips toward Boso's chest, and the juice ended up in baby's ear. Boso swallowed the remainder and said, "Oh, sorry, Little Brother! Sorry about that!" He turned the baby's head to let the juice run out of his ear. Baby didn't like having his head turned by force and he was hungry and upset because he couldn't find Ama's breast. He cried loud and hard.

"Oh, Little Brother, don't cry! I'll take care of you!"

Boso quickly chewed another bite, removed the pulp and placed his lips on baby's lips. Baby stopped crying to suck vigorously. Boso gave him that whole mouthful, bit by bit, without losing any of it., keeping his mouth right on baby's mouth.

"Look, Ama, we're getting good at it! We didn't waste any of that bite!"

"Good for you, my Son."

Boso chewed and fed his baby several bites of the cane, minus the pulp. His baby finally began to get full, stopped crying between bites, and then stopped sucking on Boso's lips.

"You're full at last, *Ame-si*. Ah, that's good. My lips are beginning to feel swollen with all that sucking you have done on them. Isn't it wonderful, *Ame-si*, that I can feed you? I don't have to ask a woman to feed you for me. I can feed you myself. Oh, joy! I'm so happy! *Nana rana-e!*" (My Love!)

Boso hugged the baby to him. "You and I can win, *Ame!* (Brother) We can lick the whole tribe. We can prove them all wrong!"

"Don't be too sure of that, Son. Babies die all the time, you know. At least half of them die. They haven't a chance against the spirits when they're so weak. How could one survive without a mother?"

"Well, we will give it a try, won't we, *Ame-si*? (Dear Little Brother) We'll give it the best we have, and then we'll try even harder yet, and maybe, just maybe, we'll keep you here on earth instead of letting you go to the spirit-land.

"Ah, you're sleepy, little one. Go to sleep, my baby. Have a sweet sleep. Have a sweet sugary sleep, *nana rana-e!*"

Boso sat staring at his baby with a far-away look in his eyes. He was dreaming of all the things they could do together when the baby got bigger, *if* he lived. But he came back to reality with a jolt.

"How long do you suppose he will sleep, Ama?"

"I don't know. But probably not as long as he would sleep on a full tummy of his mother's milk."

"I wonder how many times we will be up in the night. Maybe I ought to chew some sugar cane ahead of time, so he doesn't have to wait on me to chew it when he's hungry."

"That's a good idea. You could spit it into this length of bamboo here. And you know what? You could dilute it, say half-strength, with water. I imagine that would be better for him, anyway.

"Okay, Ama, I'll do that."

When Boso had prepared the juice he said, "I know it's not night yet, but I'm tired. I think I'll lie down beside my baby and have a nap."

"That would be wise, Son. You may be up half the night with him."

Boso curled up beside his baby. "I don't know why I am so tired," he murmured. Then he thought of how he had stood alone against the whole tribe. He remembered how his knees had tried to melt on him. He recalled his fear as he had turned and tried to run from the man who was reaching for his baby. He encircled baby and bilum with one arm. "*Nana rana-si-e*! You're all mine," he whispered. No wonder he was so tired. Maybe he did have reason, after all!

CHAPTER FIVE: BOSO'S BUSY

Baby wakened before dark, crying for another feeding. Boso roused suddenly, mindful of his responsibility. He tried dribbling the sugar and water mixture from the bamboo into his baby's mouth, but it did not work too well. Too much was being wasted as baby turned his head this way and that, searching for something on which to suck. Boso lifted the bamboo to his own lips, took a mouthful, and put his lips on baby's lips. Baby immediately began sucking and the feeding once again proceeded satisfactorily. Baby seemed to enjoy the diluted sugar juice as much as he had the full-strength juice. Again Boso's heart swelled with happiness, love, and a feeling of awesome power. He could do it! He could satisfy his baby brother's needs all by himself. If only baby would live! If only he could keep spirits from attacking his baby's soft spot. He felt the baby's fontanel with his left hand. Ah, yes, Ama-si had already put a coating of pig grease over it. He would add more.

"Can I have some pig grease, Ama? I want to put some more on my baby's soft spot. I don't want spirits attacking him."

"Yes, Son, I'll get you some."

"Oh-oh," said Boso. His legs felt suspiciously warm, and he looked down to see that they were all wet.

"Baby has wet all over me."

"You'll have to gather soft ferns to put under baby's bottom, and lots of absorbent moss to soak up his water. Nogo-Ma's bilum will soon rot with it if you don't take care of it properly."

"As soon as he has had all the sugar water he wants, I will go and find some."

"That would be good. The rain has stopped. You can shake off the ferns, and wring out the moss, and dry them here by the fire."

When baby slipped off to slumberland once again, Boso lifted the *bilum* ends, tied them, and hung them over a stick, stuck into his mother's woven *pitpit* wall. Baby was content in his bag-shaped hammock, almost as secure as he had felt in his mother's womb. When Boso was sure he was not going to cry again for a while he stood and stretched.

"I'm off to search for ferns and moss, Ama."

"There's quite a lot of soft moss just the other side of my Sugu garden, Boso. There's a little spring there where water comes up out of the ground when we've had a lot of rain."

"Okay, Ama, I'll look there." He knew where to find ferns in abundance. He picked up an empty *bilum* of his mother's as he crawled out the door.

At dusk he reentered and placed a bulging *bilum* by the fire.

"Think this will be enough, Ama?"

"Too much."

"More than I need?"

"They will dry up and the ferns will be too rough on

54

your baby's skin in a few days. You'll want to pick fresh ferns for him every other day or so. There's no need to get so many at once."

"All right. I'll learn."

Boso spread the moss and ferns out to dry on the opposite side of the fireplace. He sat down with his bamboo and another piece of sugar cane and began to prepare his baby's next feeding. When he was finished he took the grass stopper from the longer water bamboo, added water, and then put the stopper in the top of the shorter bamboo to keep the flies and roaches out of the sweet juice. Duties done, he checked on his baby, hanging in the *bilum* against the wall. Baby was sleeping peacefully. Boso lay down beside the fire. With his eyes on the flames he dreamed sweet dreams of the things he and his baby would do in the months and years ahead if baby would live. Oh, if only he would live! He had better put more lard on baby's soft-spot every day for a week, at least!

"Here come our men and boys," said a voice outside.

"Maybe they mean Tikira," said Ama. Raising her voice she called, "Are Tikira and Koiyamu and Rambua coming?"

"Somebody's coming," the voice sounded from farther up the trail. "I don't know yet who."

Boso and his mother crawled outside and stood on the trail.

Right-o! It was Tikira!

"Tikira!" called Boso excitedly.

"Ame!" returned Tikira.

"Tikira, my Son, I have missed you!" said Ama.

"Ama!"

All three hugged affectionately.

"Let's go inside, Ama. I have something to show you."

Seated by the fire, Tikira drew out from his *bilum* a tin can covered in bright red paper.

"What's that?"

"It's a *tsin*. It was *tsin-fis*, but I ate all the fish. It was so good I could not stop in time to save any for you."

"*Tsin fis*," said Boso, trying the odd-sounding words.

"*Fis* means *repali*. *Tsin* is the name of the container, but it is what is inside that I want to show you now. Look." He held out the tin at an angle so they could see inside.

"Something white," observed Boso.

"Salt. White man's salt. It's called *kusa* because it is different from our salt. Take a pinch and try it."

Boso took a pinch and touched it to his lips gingerly. His tongue came out cautiously to lick his lips. "Mmm! It's delicious!" he squealed. "Try it, Ama!"

She tried it even more slowly and fearfully than Boso.

"Oh, you're right! It *is* delicious!"

Each reached for another pinch.

"It's so soft, it just melts in your mouth," said Boso. "There are no hard crystals or bits of rock in it, like our rock salt." He reached for another pinch.

"Save some for Apa. That's all I brought. I haven't been to the *tapanda* yet."

Boso and Ama smacked their lips appreciatively. Ama handed Tikira some baked sweet potatoes.

"Guess what?"

"What?" Boso asked his brother.

"Tomorrow is Sararay. (Saturday)."

"Sararay," mimicked Boso. "What does that mean?"

"It's a name for the day. There are seven days in a week-time. So there are seven names for the seven days and then you start over again."

"What's the point?"

"It's important. Tomorrow is Sararay. The next day is Sunday. We don't have to work on Sararay and Sunday. The next day is Monday. We have to get up early before dawn and go back to work on Monday morning, back to work on the bird-landing strip."

"Sararay, Sunday, Monday. What interesting words. What's the name of today?"

"I don't know. I can't remember it. It's a hard one. I

can't pronounce it. But I did remember Sararay, Sunday and Monday. Right now they are the most important."

"You're right, and you know a lot, *Ame*. Sararay, Sunday, Monday, tsin-fis, and what did you say they call that white salt?"

"*Kusa*."

"Kusa," murmured Boso, and then he could restrain himself no longer from showing off his news.

"Guess what this is," he said as he touched the *bilum* on the wall?

Tikira pulled the side of the *bilum* back far enough to look in.

"Looks like a baby. What on earth! Did you have a baby, Ama?"

Tikira looked at his mother in consternation.

"No, I didn't. But Nogo-Ma did."

"Nogo-Ma? Tikira seemed unable to take it in.

"She died," said Boso. "She had the baby the day after you went to work on the bird-landing strip at Kagua and she died this morning."

"But how come the baby's here, Ama? Do you have milk for him?"

"Of course not. I have no milk." Ama gave one of her bare breasts a squeeze to show that it was dry. "It's your brother's doings."

"Well, I couldn't let them bury him alive. He's a nice baby and Nogo-Ma wanted him so badly. She wanted to give Apa a son as brave and great as himself, she said. How could I stand by and watch them bury him alive after she had told me that?"

"But what will you feed him?'

"Sugar juice."

"He can't chew sugar cane."

"So I chew it and spit the juice into his mouth."

"Oh, like a bird feeds her babies."

"Sort of. Sort of like a *giligala* does, but I don't swallow it and regurgitate it, of course."

"No. That would be quite an act."

Both boys laughed together.

"Sararay, Sunday, Monday," chanted Boso. He didn't want to forget those new words.

"I didn't come home last Sararay. I didn't understand then what Sararay and Sunday meant. So I just stayed at Uncle Rina's house where I stay every night anyway."

"Sararay, Sunday, Monday."

"I first went to Kagua on a Monday."

"Oh?"

"So that means the day after Monday, Nogo-Ma's baby will be two week-times."

"Week-times?"

"Yes, week-times. The men talk about week-times all the time. They all tell how many week-times they've worked. I've worked two week-times now. Four week-times make one moon, they say. I don't know for myself yet but I'm going to check it out. I'm going to see if there is a new moon when I've worked four week-times. There was a new one the night before I went to Kagua. I remember it because I went frog hunting that night. There was no rain and there was a new moon. It's the last time I've been frog hunting. I'm too tired every night at Kagua, even if there is moonlight and no rain."

"What's it like to work on the bird-landing strip?"

"Tiring. They make you keep working in the hot sun, and then in the afternoons when it rains they sometimes keep you working then too. I don't like it too well, but I do enjoy the things they give us. The *kusa* and the *tsin-fis* make it worthwhile."

The boys sat silently staring into the flames until Tikira yawned.

"Let's go to the *tapanda*, Ame. I'm tired."

"You go ahead, *Ame*. I'm going to stay here with Ama tonight in case I need help with the baby."

"Right-o. I guess you couldn't take him to the manhouse, could you. Everybody would jump down your throat every time he cried and wakened them."

"Right. And he's bound to cry. So we'll just stay with Ama."

When Tikira was gone, Boso began his chant once again.

"Sararay, Sunday, Monday, tsin-fis, kusa, week-times. I don't want to forget these new words, Ama."

"You won't. You never forget anything. Your thoughts are quicker than Tikira's. You talked younger as a baby. If you had been the one who went to Kagua you'd be telling us all seven names of the days now."

"Well, I will. Someday, somehow, I will learn all seven!'"

Boso was up with his baby so many times that night he lost count. Must be the sugar water just couldn't satisfy baby like Ama-si's milk. Each time the baby cried and Boso came groggily awake he said, "Oh, my baby, you're still alive! You didn't die!" Instead of impatience at lack of sleep he felt only gladness that his baby had energy to cry.

Boso napped with his baby half the next day and half of Sunday as well. Monday morning came and Tikira returned to Kagua's bird-landing strip. Boso regretted that he hadn't been able to learn more about the strange world of civilization but he was too tired and too busy. Days and nights were all mixed up that week. Boso was so exhausted due to the strain of living with the constant threat of his baby's starvation that he had only one driving aim. "I must harvest enough sugar cane for my baby," he said over and over.

Each time baby cried he fed him mouth to mouth and then prepared the next feeding. Each day he loved baby more and hoped harder that he would live.

One evening he was wakened by Tikira's hand on his shoulder shaking him.

"*Ame*," he said groggily.

"Wake up and see the gift I bought Ama. Red *tapa* (bark cloth)! See? They call it *laplap* (cloth)."

"Lap-lap."

"Yes, *lap-lap* is their word for *tapa*. I brought it and gave it to Ama to wear on her head. The policemen wear theirs wrapped around their bodies but I'm afraid I'd look too feminine without my *tanket* leaves and *bilum* showing."

"It's beautiful, Ame. Won't you look pretty, Ama? With that hanging from your head you will be the prettiest lady in the tribe!"

"Guess what, Ame?"

"What else? Another surprise?"

"This is Franday (Friday.)"

"Franday?"

"Yes, this is Franday night and I have returned. And guess what else? I have learned all the names of the days of a week-time now so I can say them to you."

"What are they then?"

"Sararay, Sunday, Monday, Tsoonday, Tsrinday, Ponday, Franday."

"Say them again, *Ame*, so I can learn them. I only know Sararay, Sunday, Monday."

"After Monday is Tsoonday. Tsrinday, Ponday, Franday."

Boso tried again and again to say them, each time getting Tikira to repeat them, so he could get the pronunciation correctly. The baby cried and Boso reached for his bamboo of sugar-water.

"Keep saying them while I feed my baby. The more I hear them the better I will remember them."

Tikira watched Boso feed his charge, mouth to mouth, as he chanted the names of the days.

"I have worked at Kagua three week-times and the baby has lived with you a whole week-time now."

"Yes, one whole week-time. Days and nights are so mixed up I can't keep track. I sleep almost as much in the day as I do at night. I sleep when he sleeps."

"What's Naki have to say about that?"

"Naki? Oh, he has come to call me to play a few times

but he could see I was either too tired or too busy."

"Busy? Feeding him, you mean?" "Feeding him, or preparing his feeding, or cleaning up his messes, or gathering moss or ferns or harvesting sugar cane."

"Oh, I see. There's a lot of work in taking care of a baby, isn't there?"

"There surely is. I don't see how women make all the gardens for all of us to eat and have babies and raise them at the same time. Of course they don't have to prepare feeding like I do. They have milk on demand."

Baby cried and Boso hurried to take another mouthful of sugar water.

"Yes, that would make it quite a bit easier. At least they can talk while they nurse their babies. You can't. Well, at least your ears aren't busy. You can listen. I have something to tell you. I saw a white man today."

Boso jerked his head up, swallowed the remaining juice and exclaimed, "Really? What did he look like?"

"Well, I didn't get to see him very closely. There were crowds of people around him. But what I saw was very strange."

"Go on, tell me," said Boso as baby cried and he had to take another mouthful.

"There's no way anybody could understand his speech. There wasn't one intelligible word in it! He sounded like a bird. His whole body was covered with *lap-lap, tapa*, like Ama's here only more the color of his skin. He looked rather naked with no *tanket* leaves in back or *bilum* netting in front. His face and hands were really white or red; not brown at all. His hair wasn't like hair at all, more like threads, bark threads. Actually, it reminded me most of a cassowary's tail. But his feet! Now his feet were something else!"

Tikira paused thoughtfully.

"What was different about his feet?" urged Boso.

"Well, I studied his footprints after he went back to the

house and I could almost believe what some people say. They say he's a spirit and maybe he is… because… he doesn't have any toes! His feet must be huge, as big as those footprints were! And long, very long!. Why, you know, Ama is always saying I have long feet but I could fit one of my feet and half of the other one into his footprint. But even though it was so long, there still wasn't the print of any toes. Just imagine how much longer it would have been if he had had toes!"

"Think of it," responded Boso. "A toeless creature! And you've seen it! Why, even pigs have two toes. And cassowaries have three and marsupials have five. Who would have believed? A creature with no toes. Some call him a man and he doesn't have any toes. What did his hands look like?"

"He had big hands and fingers like ours. Different times I saw him pointing here and there as he was giving directions about the bird-landing strip and I would guess he has five fingers on each hand just like you and me. But people who were closer to him say he has bristles on his hands, and fingers, like you see on a pig's back."

"Bristley hands, toeless feet and hair like thread, bark thread. I can't imagine such a creature. What were his eyes like?"

"I didn't see his eyes close enough to tell, but Uncle Rina has and he says they're cooled-off eyes like people have when their eyes have been hit by an exploding hot stone, heated for a *mumu*, you know. They aren't brown like ours, he said."

"But cooled-off eyes are blind. Can this bristly-handed, toeless footed creature see?"

"He must be able to see. Nobody led him around like a blind person. How could he know where to point and give directions if he couldn't see?"

"Where did he come from?"

"He walked in over the mountains from a mountain called Mount Ialibu. Uncle Rina says that's where all the policemen walk in from. There's a bird-landing strip at Mount Ialibu. This spirit-man, or whatever he is, landed there in one of the big birds."

"He probably is a spirit then. Someone said those big birds come bringing cargo from the spirits of our ancestors. If he was in one, he must be from the spirit world too.

"If he's a spirit of one of our ancestors, why can't he talk intelligibly? Why can't we understand him?"

"Maybe he has been so long in the spirit world that he has forgotten our language. Maybe they don't speak it there. How did everybody get his directions about the bird-landing strip if nobody understood him? Do you just go by his motions and pointing?"

"No, there's a man from Mt. Ialibu called a 'turn-him-talk.' He turns the toeless creature's words into our language."

"How did he learn their language? Was he spirit-instructed?"

"I don't know. Maybe I will get to see him better next week-time. Somebody said he is going to stay at Kagua several days."

"Learn all you can about him and tell me. See if you can't get closer to him next week-time, won't you?"

"I don't know. Maybe. I was sort of scared of him today, if you know what I mean. I didn't want to get too close. But I guess he didn't try to grab anyone or eat anyone. I've heard rumors that white men do eat people canned in tsins just like fish."

"Really?"

"Yes, somebody said friends of theirs had been to Mt. Ialibu where there's a whole family of these toeless creatures ~ man, woman and children. And these friends of theirs saw them taking tsins off the big bird with pictures of babies on them."

"So they think they're eating babies?"

"Yes. You know the tsin-fis I brought you last week

had that red wrapper around it with a picture of a fish on it? And that's what was inside the tsin. Fish. So when they put a picture of a baby on the outside it must be the flesh of babies on the inside."

"I guess that must be." Boso hugged his baby, *bilum* and all to his chest.

'Oh, Baby, I'm going to keep you away from those toeless creatures! No bristle-hands are going to grab my baby!"

Monday, Tsoonday, Tsrinday, the days flew by because Boso was so busy. The specter of starvation hanging over his baby was again staring him in the face. Ama's sugar cane garden was fast being depleted. What would baby do when there was no more sugar cane?

"Grow, sugar cane, grow!" He stood in front of the young cane plants and lectured them every time he went to one of his mother's gardens to harvest another stick of sugar cane. He became doubly careful to extract every milliliter of juice from the pulp for his baby. He grew fanatical about not letting anyone else eat any sugar cane. No matter how much Tikira or Naki or anyone else begged him or his mother for sugar cane, he refused.

"No! We must save it all for the baby! There's so much you can eat. There's so little to keep him alive!"

Tikira, Koiyamu and Rambua all came together to visit Boso and his baby on Saturday afternoon. They had a story to tell.

"Hi, Boys, did you see the white man this week?" greeted Boso.

"We certainly did," answered Koiyamu. "We saw him three times. Every time he came out on the bird-landing strip we tried to get as close to him as we could. We listened to his funny bird talk and we tried to repeat some of the sounds. We looked him over closely and saw the tapa or lap-lap didn't cover his knees and thighs. They have bristles on them just like his hands."

"Did you get a good look at his toeless feet?"

"We tried, but they were so covered with mud that we couldn't see why there weren't any toes. Must be mud sticks to his feet worse than ours. Of course ours get all muddy too when we're working on the bird strip but we can still see the shape of our feet through the mud. We couldn't his."

"But wait, Boso. You have to hear the story Rambua has to tell," said Tikira.

"My ears are wide open, waiting," grinned Boso.

"One day the turn-him-talk from Mt. Ialibu was directing a work crew near me. I thought up a question to ask him about my work, and after he had come to me and answered me, I asked him the real question I had. I said, "These white men whose talk you turn, are they like real men? Are they put together the same way we are?

"He laughed and said, 'No, maybe not. There's quite a tale I can tell you about one of them. This one white man was overseeing two tribes of men working on two different ends of a road. He was anxious to get the road finished so he could bring in his *karo* that rolls on four round legs.'"

"*Karo*? What's a *karo*?"

"I don't know, but when they have one they don't have to walk anywhere. They sit in it, and it rolls on these four round legs and carries them along.

"So anyway, he wanted these two tribes to work fast and get this road done. But every time he left the first tribe to go to oversee the second's work, the first tribe would sit down, make a fire, and start visiting. When he left the second tribe to go back to the first, the second tribe would make a fire and start roasting sweet potatoes. He got so worn out trying to rush back and forth to oversee both tribes that the sweat was pouring down his red face and dripping off his chin. So guess what he did?"

"He got another white man to oversee one tribe," suggested Boso.

"Wrong. He took out one of his eyes and laid it on a

stump."

Boso clicked his thumbnail off his two front teeth. "He took out his own eye?"

"Yes."

"But how could he do that?"

"I don't know. He must be made different than we are. Anyway, he laid this eye on a stump and said, 'My eye will be watching you to see if you keep working or go sit by the fire.' So the men of both tribes worked hard for two days. But then one afternoon a man working under the watchful eye said, 'I'm tired of working so hard without a break to straighten my back,' so he crept up behind the eye and stuck his hat over it. They had half a day's leisure by the fire. When the white man came and found the hat over his eye, he was terribly angry. He and his policeman went after them with clubs. He threw the hat in the fire, and guess what he did next?"

"Took off his ear and put it by his eye, and said he would hear the next one that came near his eye?"

"No, but you're on the right trail! He took out his teeth and set them by his eye and said they'd bite anyone who came near the eye."

Boso clicked his thumbnail again He shook his right hand, swiveling it on the wrist, up by his right shoulder in sheer astonishment. "Oh, no! This can't be a true story!"

"The turn-him-talk said it is true. He said he has often seen his white man take out his teeth."

"O-my-father! Are they spirits or men or monsters?"

"We don't know, but the turn-him-talk said there was nothing for it then but for both tribes to work. They did. They finished the road. Now the white man sits in his karo and rolls by on round feet without walking."

"O-my-father!" exclaimed Boso fluttering his fingers by his shoulder again.

"This is all too much for my understanding. What sort of creatures are they that they can commandeer big birds to fly them through the sky, and round-legged karo creatures to carry them on the ground and take out their eyes and teeth to see and bite people far away from them? I wonder if they aren't worse than stonemen or evil spirits?"

"But they don't kill, Boso. The turn-him-talk says they are only angry when black men don't work. Otherwise they are friendly, and give out cargo, and laugh and joke with us."

"Strange. I wonder how long before I see one for myself. I suppose not until baby's walking and talking at least." Then his liver tried to come up into his throat and choke him again when he remembered Ama's sugar cane was running out. Baby would probably never live to walk and talk and see a white man. Baby wasn't doing too well, these days. He didn't cry much. He seemed to be saving all his small store of strength for sucking on Boso's lips.

CHAPTER SIX: SUGAR CANE SHORTAGE

"Here, Baby, let me change your moss and ferns and then we will go see Apa. This is the last stick of sugar cane here, and I dare not wait any longer to ask Apa what we will do."

Boso changed his baby's moss and ferns and picked every little piece of dried fern from baby's back and tummy, hair and face.

"We have to get you all cleaned up to see Apa. We have to look as nice as we can."

Boso deftly lifted, adjusted and tied the *bilum* on his back. He was getting very good at handling a baby in a *bilum*. He patted baby's bottom through the *bilum* as he crouched and crawled through the low doorway. Outside he stood erect and stretched without letting go of the *bilum* ends. He walked quickly to the *tapanda*.

Men and boys were sitting around the fire listening to a Sumbura man recount the tale of his last hunt. Boso sat down near his father without a word. It was impolite to interrupt. But oh, how hard it was to be patient through all the boring details. What does it matter how he moved his arm or did this or that when my baby may be dying, thought Boso. At last the great hunter needed the whole outside for a demonstration. Everyone followed him out except Apa and Boso. At last they were alone. Now he had the desired silence and his father's full attention. But his liver was swelling so he could hardly talk.'

"Apa."

"My son."

"I've brought my baby to show you." Boso untied the bilum knot at his chest and brought it around to lay on his lap. He pulled back the *bilum* and displayed his baby.

Apa stared silently at the child. Boso willed himself to match his father's self-control. The lump dissolved in his throat and he wanted to talk. Why was patience so hard to come by?

At last Apa murmured, "He's still alive."

"Yes, Apa, he's still alive. And he's growing, you see. At least his head and stomach are larger. His arms and legs are getting thinner all the time, but they are growing longer."

"How long has it been, I wonder."

"One moon and a few days."

"How do you know? Surely you didn't have time to watch the moon, as busy as you must have been?"

"Tikira said there was a new moon the night before he went to Kagua. Baby was born the day after he left. Tikira is very aware of time since he went to Kagua. He has learned that seven days make a week-time and he's even learned the name of every day."

"And so?"

"Baby is six week-times now. His little mother died before he was two week-times."

"Week-times, eh? You sound like you know what you are talking about."

"Yes, Apa. Four week-times have finished Ama's sugar cane gardens. I'm getting desperate. I'm about ready to go out and steal sugar cane. But I thought I would come and tell you about my problem first."

"Well done, Son. I don't want you to lose your fingers for stealing. Have you grown tired of this huge responsibility you have undertaken?"

"No, Apa. I'm not tired at all. I'm just worried that after all now, Baby is going to have to die for lack of sugar cane."

"That's all you've fed him? No woman has given him any milk?"

"No. No milk. He has had only sugar cane and water."

"There is a solution to your problem."

"Yes, Apa?"

"I'm proud of you, Son. You make my liver quiver and swell with happiness. You may have all the sugar cane in all my wives' gardens."

"Apa! *ALL* your wives'?"

"Yes. Begin with the baby's mother's gardens. When they are gone, you may help yourself to the gardens of my other three wives."

"O-my-father! Oh, Apa-YO! Baby, you hear? You hear? You don't have to die! We have lots of sugar cane! Lots! Oh, Apa. *You* make *my* liver quiver and swell with happiness! Before it was swollen with fear and sorrow. Now it's a good quivering, a good swelling! It feels good inside."

"Here. Give me the baby. Go get a stick of sugar cane and show me this feeding process."

"Right-o, Apa. Here you go, Baby! You're going to lie in our Apa's lap. And do you know who our Apa is? He's the Great Warrior, Mambi, the Invincible, the Indestructible!"

"Oh-ho! Baby can't hear you."

"Why, sure he can, Apa. I talk to him all the time. Sometimes I *know* he is listening.

"Oh, yes, he has ears. But he can't understand. He doesn't have thoughts."

"Nevermind. I will give him my thoughts. I will put my

thoughts into his ears and into his head. But you can talk to him while I'm gone. You can put your great thoughts into him."

"No, I'll save mine for men and boys who can think. But more important, is he likely to wet all over me?"

"No, I hope not.

"You wouldn't do that, would you, Baby? Not to our great Apa?

"I just put fresh ferns and moss under him, Apa. They should absorb everything. Or would you rather I take him with me?"

"No. Be off. Go get that sugar cane."

"I'm going."

Naki and some of the other boys gathered around as Boso demonstrated the feeding process to Apa.

"You have kept him alive a long time, Boso," said Naki.

"You're both father and mother to him," said another.

"We're missing you in our play, Boso," said Naki. "It's been a long time since you've played with us. It's not nearly as much fun without you. Makira's tribe beat our tribe in a mock battle yesterday. They wouldn't have won if you had been there. They really made fun of us. They said, 'The sons of the Kati-loma can't say *Kati* any more. You're all *kale nakinu* instead of *kati nakinu*. You're all orphans. When you grow up your tribe will be weak. There won't be any more Kati-loma in the land."

Boso lifted his lips from his baby's to say, "Oh, no, we can't have that, can we? Have you planned the next battle?"

"Yes, we've planned a mud fight three days from now."

"Well, I'll have to plan on joining you. Maybe I can get Grandpa or somebody to babysit for me."

"I think some such can be arranged," said Apa. "We can't have the name of the Kati-loma dragged in the mud! If Boso can give all his time to keep this little man alive, Kaisuwa and I can babysit now and then. I was going to say I might even try my hand at feeding him. But I guess I should say my mouth, not my hand, shouldn't I?"

"Have you seen my new baby brother, Boso?" asked Naki.

"No, I haven't. How is he doing?"

"Fine. Just fine. How about coming to see him when you leave here.?"

Boso spent all day at the tapanda, visiting with the boys and men, and feeding baby all the sugar juice he could hold. Rain clouds threatened at mid-afternoon and Naki said, "Ama will be home now any time, Boso. Let's go to her house so you can see our baby."

Naki-Ma was peeling sweet potatoes, with a well-carved bamboo knife, when the boys arrived.

"Ama, I've brought Boso to show him our baby. He's never seen him yet."

"No, you haven't, have you, Boso?" responded Naki-Ma as the two boys sat down by the fireplace. "You've been so busy mothering your own baby brother, you haven't had time to look at any other babies."

She laid down her bamboo knife and swung her *bilum* from her head around to her lap. She opened the *bilum* to show a nice chubby brown baby.

"Oh, isn't he fat and nice!" exclaimed Boso.

"Yes, he is," agreed Naki-Ma as the baby opened his mouth wide and cried to protest the interruption of his nap. Naki-Ma filled the wide opened mouth with her breast and muffled the baby's howl. He immediately began to suck.

Boso couldn't help thinking how convenient and easy it would be to feed a baby if he were a woman. Nevermind, he told himself brusquely. I wouldn't be a woman if I could. Imagine never going out to battle. Imagine always staying behind to dig in the dirt. What a boring life women have! I'm glad I'm a boy even though I have to work harder to save my baby's life.

"Let me see your baby," asked Naki-Ma.

Boso untied his bilum from his shoulders and brought it around to open on his lap.

"Oh, he has a cute little face. And look at those black eyebrows and all of that black hair!"

Boso looked at her baby's hair and brows. He had thinner brown hair and no obvious eyebrows yet.

"Yes, he's a nice baby. Far too nice to waste! I couldn't bear to see him buried with his mother."

"Our baby's bigger and fatter, but your baby has more hair," observed Naki.

"Yours was born before mine," Boso hastened to remind his friend.

"Yes, that's true. I was already back here at my own house before Nogo-Ma went to the bush," agreed Naki-Ma.

"I feared my Baby might have to die," confided Boso to Naki-Ma. "We have finished all of Ama's sugar cane. But Apa told me this morning I can have all of his wives' sugar cane. My baby will get fatter now. I won't have to dilute the sugar cane juice with as much water as I have been doing."

"That's good. I'm glad you have all you need now. You're working hard and I do like to see a hard-working boy!"

Apa and Kaisuwa babysat for Boso while he pelted the 'enemy' with mud. Boso fought long and hard, determined to avenge the sneers and restore glory to the *Kati-loma naki-nu*. All and sundry must know now and forever that the Kati-loma would not be defeated. Some day he and his baby would take their father's place and stand invincible, indestructible and undefeated as Mambi had stood while so many other men died. Boso and his friends won the mud fight. They defeated the other tribe so completely that they didn't challenge them again for many moons.

"We did it, Boso! We did it! With your help we wiped them out! Now let's go play tops," invited Naki.

"No, boys, no tops for me now. I've got to get back to

my baby."

"Oh, that baby! That's all we hear about any more," howled a boy named Su. "How you work and take care of that baby! Forget him for one day. Let someone else take care of him. Come and play tops. Don't you want lots of *pandanus* nuts?"

"Sure I want lots of nuts. But I don't have the time to play tops now."

"Sissy Boso, acts like a woman, taking care of her baby," taunted Su.

"How dare you? Who just helped you beat the Sakamapi boys? How can I be a sissy and fight like that?"

"But you are a sissy. You spend all your time doing a woman's work."

Boso was ready to let fly with his fists at this disgusting boy of his own tribe when it seemed he heard his little Ama-si's words, "Your father is a great man. He is self-controlled. He never beats…"

Boso dropped his fists. "I could flatten you," he said.

"Go ahead, Sissy. Try it," taunted the bigger boy.

"Let him be, Su." Commanded Naki. "He left his baby to help us with this mud battle. Now you leave him alone."

Boso left while someone was on his side. "The ungrateful wretch," he muttered as he hurried homeward. "Why is Naki the only one who appreciates me? Maybe I should have let Su get tromped in the mud! It'd serve him right!"

Another month of sugar cane feedings went by and still Boso's baby was no fatter. Again he visited Naki-ma to compare babies. He was astonished at how much her baby had grown.

"I can't make my baby fat," he confided in despair. "His head and tummy grow, but his legs and arms don't."

"His legs and arms are growing longer," she observed, "but they're just not filling out."

The babies lay on their pandanus leaf-mats in the *bilums* side by side on the bamboo floor. Boso groaned aloud as he compared them.

"My baby's so skinny. Only his head is big and his tummy is swollen Is he going to die?"

"Who can say? But he's certainly very much alive right now. He moves around a lot more than my baby. He's very active and observant. See how he follows you with his eyes?"

Boso had only been comparing size, he realized. Now he compared movements. Yes, his baby moved far more and was definitely more alert to what was taking place around him. He turned his eyes to the person speaking. Boso stood up and walked to the other side of the hut. Baby turned his head to keep Boso in sight. Naki's baby brother lay there without moving.

"You see that? He turned his head so he could keep watching you. My baby hardly pays any attention to me or you."

Boso's baby had turned his head again to look at the woman as she talked. As soon as she was done speaking, however, he turned his head back again and fastened his eyes on Boso.

"My Baby!" Boso swooped down on him. Baby gurgled laughter. "You wonderful baby! You know me and you love me! You put your thoughts on me! I know you do! Apa and everyone else says you don't have any thoughts. But I knew you were listening and this proves it! You listen and you have thoughts, and you put your thoughts on me! You know I care about you, and you care about me!"

He hugged his baby, *bilum* and all, to his bare chest. Baby gurgled and cooed.

"See how hard he tries to talk, Naki-Ma? I know he has thoughts and he wants to say them to me. But he can't yet. But he will, some day. Just wait. He will talk to me. Oh, I can't wait to hear what he has to say! I just can't wait!"

"You'll have to," the woman was saying as Naki and a couple of his playmates burst in the low door.

"Boso! Boso! You're here! Come and play tops with us.

The pandanus nuts are growing bigger. They'll soon be ready to harvest, the first ones, anyway. I know the spirits are pleased with how much we play, and how well we play. But you've only played twice. Come on."

"I can't," Boso began. "I have to watch my baby. And besides, I didn't bring my tops with me. I made…"

"Go ahead, Boso. Play with the boys. Give your baby a feeding of sugar cane and then go play with the boys. He will be all right here with me and my baby while you play."

"You can use one of my tops," offered Naki.. "Apa made me two new ones, and they spin just fine."

"Okay, Naki. I'll play with you. Just let me feed my baby first."

Baby ate until he was sleepy. When his eyes shut to stay, for a while, Boso slipped away with the boys.

He took his stance between Naki on his left, and two boys on his right, facing a second team of four about eight feet away. Each boy had a *pitpit* cane stuck upright in the clay in front of him. They spun their tops between the palms of their hands, throwing them at the same time. Boso could make his top land and spin around his opponent's cane more often than any boy his size.

"We won! We won!" yelled Naki, pounding Boso on the back. "The spirits are pleased with your prowess this afternoon and will give you a good nut harvest," he said, repeating the exact words his father had said to him the day before.

Boso hurried back to his baby. Alone with him, in his mother's hut, he crooned over him. "Oh, Baby, you made me so happy today when you showed both Naki's mother and me how you put your thoughts on me.

Baby gurgled in response.

Boso took both Baby's hands in his. Immediately baby tried to pull himself up.

"Ama says I shouldn't let you do that. She says you'll break your neck. But I just wonder if she might be wrong. You're so strong, and you move so much more than a baby bigger than you. Maybe you want to sit up and look around. If people are wrong about you having thoughts, they might be wrong about your neck.

Boso let Baby pull himself forward. Boso held his arms stiff and Baby pulled against him until he was nearly in a sitting position. They played this game for several days alone, before they showed Ama.

"He'll break his neck!" Ama screamed in consternation.

"He's been doing it for days, and he hasn't broken it yet," defied Boso. He picked him up out of the *bilum* and set him on his lap. Baby leaned his bare back against Boso's bare tummy, and they sat there, nice and cozy, by the fire.

"He's too young to be out of the *bilum*," argued Ama.

"He's strong. Naki-Ma says he moves more, and is more observant than her baby, and it's true.

Ama handed Boso a warm sweet potato after slapping the ashes off it. Boso slapped it a couple more times, then took a big bite. Baby reached for the sweet potato in Boso's hand.

"Oh, Ama, look! He wants some sweet potato."

"He's too young, of course, but take a little bit of the softest part right in the center. Mash it between your fingers a bit, then put it in his mouth and see what he does."

Boso did. Baby gummed it. Some drooled back out of his mouth but he sucked and smacked his lips together and tried hard to get it down. Boso mashed more, and baby ate it, enthusiastically.

"I think I could mash some well-cooked sweet potato with a pestle and mix it with my sugar and water. I think he would eat it, Ama. I just think he would!"

"You're probably right."

In this way, Boso added a third ingredient to his baby's regular diet. The sweet potato was more substantial and satisfied his baby for longer. Now he could go longer between feedings.

"Nuts! Nuts! And more nuts! Have you ever seen a better nut harvest?" Apa asked Kaisuwa as Boso sat in the tapanda with them, cracking the pandanus nuts between his strong teeth, his baby cuddled in front of him.

"You men really played the tops well this time," complimented Kaisuwa. "I don't know as I ever saw a better nut harvest. Why, I haven't hardly eaten a sweet potato for days! It feels so much better to have a bellyful of nuts!"

Boso's Baby reached for the nuts in Boso's hand.

"No, Baby! No nuts for you! You'd choke on them! We can't mash them to a soft paste like we can sweet potatoes."

Boso reached behind him for a stick of sugar cane. He peeled one section with his teeth, split it into quarters and put one quarter into his baby's hand. Baby loved gumming a piece of sugar cane now that he could almost sit alone and hold it in his own little hand. He would probably cut his first teeth some day on sugar cane.

"What a funny little man he is," observed the men. "Such a big head and such a big stomach! But what skinny arms and legs! You funny little man!"

The next day a baby from Katiloma and a baby from Sakamapi died. Fear gripped Boso's heart as he listened to the wail of the bereft mother. A few hours later when the wail of the second mother rose from the nearby hill, he felt the fear was going to suffocate him.

"The spirits are after our babies, Apa. What if they take mine? What can I do?"

"There's nothing to do, Son. You can try putting more lard on baby's soft spot. The father of the baby who died here this morning, said the child had had diarrhea for days. Once a baby gets diarrhea they die fast. Lots of us have diarrhea now, but most of us older ones will survive it. Babies and little children can't, however."

The next week Apa began work on the Kagua bird-landing strip, walking the ten miles to Kagua each Monday morning, and home again each *Franday* night.

"We can be thankful the policemen are keeping us all busy on this bird-landing strip," said Apa. "Otherwise some tribe would decide now is the time to take their revenge for our earlier attacks on them. Now, while our ranks are so depleted by our first defeat."

"Yes, the bird-landing strip has its advantages, I suppose," agreed the other man. The fish in tsin cans, the salt, the beads and the laplaps are sure nice things to have. But I'd rather go back to the good old lazy days when a policeman wasn't standing over me yelling his lungs raw."

Boso visited Naki and his mother one afternoon when he was feeling lonesome for Apa and Tikira.'

"What happened to your baby?" he asked, shocked to see how thin and emaciated the once fat baby now was.

"He's had diarrhea for days," said Naki-Ma. "We all have. But we can take it. Baby can't. He's lost all his fat. Five babies have died now, and I suppose mine will too. He doesn't even want to nurse."

Naki-Ma cracked another nut and ate it. (She never had a thought that the rich nut diet was causing her own diarrhea and making her milk so strong that it was harming her baby. None of the tribe realized it. People so starved for protein can be harmed by that very protein when they take it in unlimited quantities to the exclusion of all other food.)

"Why are the spirits so angry at us? Why are they taking all of our babies?" asked Boso.

"I don't know. I can't understand. How is your baby? Has he had diarrhea?"

"No, he hasn't. He's the same as always." Boso took his baby from the bilum and sat him between his legs, leaning against him.

"Why, he can sit up!"

"Almost." He handed Baby a quarter section of sugar cane and Baby began gumming it happily.

"Look! He can chew sugar cane all by himself!"

"Not really. He doesn't have any teeth yet so he is not actually chewing it. He is just gumming it."

"But he knows how to suck in the juice! Look at that!"

"Yes, he's learning, but he lets a lot of juice run out. His tummy gets awful sticky and so do his hands and arms."

"But look how strong he is!"

"Yes, but his arms and legs are still skinny."

"But at least he has a nice fat tummy. Look at my baby. He has no tummy left. No fat anywhere."

"Maybe you should give him some water," suggested Boso. "When I have diarrhea like now, I get so thirsty for water all the time. I drink and drink."

"I don't think he'd drink it. He won't even nurse. But I guess I could try. Water sure hasn't hurt your baby, has it? Maybe I ought to try a little sugar juice and water together."

Nut season finally came to an end and people returned to their regular diet. To Boso and Naki's joy and delight, both of their babies survived the nut season. But now the boys were pestering Boso once again to do things with them. One night Boso asked Ama if Baby could stay with her while he joined the boys in a frog hunt in the moonlight.

Boso cooked his frogs and shared them with Ama while Baby slept. When he was full and satisfied he picked up his Baby and cuddled him against his tummy with his back to the fireplace. Baby drew up his legs between their tummies and Boso laughed aloud.

"You draw your skinny little legs up just like a frog, Baby. I think I ought to call you Dindi."

Boso's baby was christened.

"Are you sure he is strong enough for a name, Boso?"

"I don't know, Ama, but in some ways he is stronger than other babies. So many babies have died in the last two moons but mine didn't."

"I know. That's what I mean. You give him a name and

the spirits are sure to find him. Better let him go nameless a little longer and maybe they can't locate him. You don't want to flaunt his life in their faces when so many babies have died."

"Okay, Ama. I won't call him by name out loud."

However, in the next several weeks he thought of his baby as Dindi, and he even whispered it in his ear as he cuddled him by night and by day.

"You're my little Dindi. You're the nicest little Dindi a boy ever had. You set your thoughts on me, and I set my thoughts on you. My Dindi, my little Dindi-si."

Boso carried his baby out all the time now.

"Put your baby down and come play," the boys teased.

"No, I'm busy," said Boso, turning away.

"Oh, go on, then! Your mother's calling you," they called, using a favorite childish taunt. When Boso didn't respond they changed it to, "Baby, your mama's calling you!"

"Stop it! Stop it!" screamed Boso in instant rage. "His mother is **not** calling him!" Baby's mother had gone to the spirit world. If she were calling him from there, that meant his baby would die!

"He has a mother!" screamed Boso, stamping his foot viciously. "My mother is his mother! So you all shut your mouths!"

CHAPTER SEVEN: HUNTING

Now that the boys had learned how they could make Boso angry, some of them taunted him every time he refused to join them in a swim or a battle or at play.

"Baby, your mother's calling you," they chanted.

Boso's rages seemed to accomplish nothing.

"Let's go away, Dindi," he whispered in his baby's ear. "They even come here to Ama's house to tease us. Let's us two go right away from here!. Let's go to the bush. We'll take sugar cane and sweet potatoes and go deep into the bush and stay out there for a while. We'll hunt possum and wallaby and cockatoo. Oh, Dindi, you don't know how good things taste!"

Boso gathered his bow and arrows and spear, Dindi's *bilum* and an extra *bilum* of his mother's and went to her garden with Dindi riding piggy back on his shoulders.

"Ama, Dindi and I are going away to the bush for a while. Some of the children keep saying that Dindi's mother is calling him because they're mad at me for not spending all of my time playing with them. So Dindi and I are going away for a few days. May I get sweet potatoes from you? Then I will go to Apa's gardens to get sugar cane and we'll be off. Don't look for us until you see us coming. The way I feel now we'll be gone a long time. But I can't say for sure because I don't know how Dindi will take to bush life."

"Here's a *bilumful* of sweet potatoes I had dug already. Take all you want. I can dig more. You'd better take my umbrella as well as Dindi's little one and your own. Will you carry a live coal or will you start your own fire?"

"I'll start my own. I won't want to make a fire until I have built a shelter and done some hunting so I'll just start my own."

Boso transferred as many sweet potatoes as he thought they could use in the next few days to the billum he had brought along.

"*Patepe, Ama-nde,*" he rhymed, putting the love suffix on the end of mother.

"*Patepullapape, nana naki lapo-si.* (Good-by my two dear little boys,)" called Ama.

Boso stopped by Apa's most distant bush garden and cut several big sticks of sugar cane. He cut them into arm length and put them into Dindi's *bilum* with both umbrellas. He tied the *bilum* of sweet potatoes around his shoulders first. Secondly he tied on Dindi's smaller billum.

"Up you go, Dindi. It's a good thing you've learned to ride on my shoulders so well because there's no room in that *bilum* until we take your sugar cane out."

Boso hoisted Dindi up to sit on his shoulders, over the two *bilums*, then picked up his bow and arrows one by one with the toes of his left foot and retrieved them with his right hand. By using his left foot as a third hand he did not have to bend too far forward and risk dislodging Dindi or one of the *bilums*. His left hand supported Dindi's back, pressing him and two *bilums* against the back of his head.

"Now my spear, and here we go, Dindi. Off on our first hunt together. Someday we'll be great hunters like Apa. You're getting an early start, Dindi, my boy. I never went on a hunt until I was big enough to walk the whole way and carry my own little bow and arrows. Here you're going on your first hunt before you can even walk."

Dindi had caught Boso's excitement and he chattered and cooed on Boso's shoulders just like a little monkey.

Sometime later when they were in deep jungle Boso whispered, "Let's not talk any more now, Dindi. Let's be real quiet and maybe I will see something to shoot before I even choose a spot for our shelter. Sh-sh now, let's be real quiet. *Pawa-si, pawa-si.*"

Boso sneaked stealthily along as well as he might with such a big load on his slight shoulders and back. Again Dindi caught his mood and remained quiet most of the time. Perhaps the deep jungle felt eerie to him. Perhaps he couldn't understand the duskiness of the total foliage cover changing noon day brightness to a strange green light. Anyway, his chatter subsided and he clung silently to Boso's kinky head.

At last Boso stopped, dropped his weapons and lifted Dindi from his shoulders to a triangle of moss.

"This spot will do as well as any, Dindi," he whispered, "and I'm tired of this load. He took off both *bilums* and tied them to a little sapling. He stretched and bent and flexed his back and shoulders and arm muscles, then crouched on the moss beside Dindi, with his bow and arrows in his hands.

"We've got to be real quiet," he whispered with his lips right up against Dindi's ear, and one index finger over Dindi's lips. "If you'll be real quiet maybe I can get us some meat."

Subdued by Boso's strange behavior as well as sitting on a seat of moss, surrounded by thick foliage, Dindi leaned silently into Boso's side, as he sat beside him, until he began to feel sleepy. Boso felt him relax against him, and when the baby slept soundly he eased him back onto the moss, and picked up his bow and an arrow.

He rose and tip-toed a few feet away. Keeping his baby in sight, he silently scanned every nook and cranny of the dense jungle foliage. Finally a movement caught his eye. He stood like a statue till the marsupial came in range of his bow. Still he waited as it drew closer. There was no hurry. It was easy to be patient. He had the perfect shot and he took it.

With glee he gutted his kill, gathered wood for a fire, and started it by pulling a length of *kundu* cane against dry wood held between his toes. The friction caused by the continuous rubbing finally created sparks which he caught in the dried grasses and leaves placed under his foot. He cupped these dried grasses in his hands and blew on them carefully until he had enticed a small flame which he then placed under his dried twigs.

The meat was cooking and their brush arbor shelter was half built before Dindi awakened from his nap.

"How's my little Dindi? Look. We've got us some marsupial cooking here but it's not ready yet. You're hungry, aren't you? I'll get you some sugar juice and sweet potato."

Boso fed him the sugar juice first. Now that Dindi could sit up so well, he sat in Boso's lap and took whole mouthfuls of juice at once from Boso's lips. Because the sweet potato was cold Boso chewed it up some before putting it into Dindi's mouth. When Dindi's hunger had subsided a little Boso split him a quarter of a sugar cane section.

"Here you go, Dindi, You can gum this now. You don't want to get too full before the meat's done. You want to be at least a little hungry for your first meal of meat. I'm going to finish our shelter while you eat your sugar cane. We've been real lucky. The rain has held off longer than some days. Looks like I can get this finished before it comes."

Boso chattered to Dindi as always while he worked.

"It's a good thing I have helped the bigger boys make so many of these shelters in the past. I'm good at it now, Dindi. We'll have a tip-top little hut here in no time.

Before the rain comes we'll be snug and cozy in our little waterproof cubbyhole. Look at those ferns over there. I'll make a nice soft bed of them. We are going to have to go somewhere else to get some stones for our fireplace, though. We can look for mushrooms at the same time.

"I'm just going over here a little ways to get some more vines for tying brush to my walls. Can you see me, Dindi? Watch me. Talk to me."

Dindi chattered as he always did when Boso asked him questions. None of the sounds made any sense, but they both felt like they were sharing, if not exactly communicating.

"Thatta boy! That's my baby! Dindi's going to be a great hunter someday. He's already learning to be content in the bush, aren't you, Dindi?"

When the shelter was completed and the outside fire replenished, Boso hoisted Dindi to his shoulders once again.

"Off we go again to find some stones, and maybe some mushrooms and *rani*, too. The meat is probably done, but we'll wait because we want to find these things before it rains."

Stones were easy to find and bring, to make the fireplace. They went farther afield to look for mushrooms and greens."

"Look, Dindi, our meat is done. While it cools a bit we will transfer some of these coals into our new fireplace inside. I'll set you right here out of the way, so you don't get burned. It's hot! I'm going to carry hot coals inside. Hot! Hot! You don't want to get burned!"

At last all was in order. They sat by their fire. Boso cut Dindi a leg of marsupial. He blew on it a little and held it against his own lips to make sure it wasn't too hot.

"It's meat, Dindi, meat! Your first meat!"

Dindi liked the taste of it. He sucked on it and gummed it happily. Boso ate his fill, saving the fattiest pieces for Dindi, because it was evident that the baby liked the fat.

Dindi held out his hand for more and said, "*Gi.*"

" *Gi*! Oh, Dindi, you said '*Gi*!' That's your first real word besides a-ma-ma-ma and a-pa-pa-pa. Oh, my Dindi! You said '*gi*' and Ama isn't even here to hear it! Wait until I tell her! Won't she be happy? You don't even have any teeth yet and you're already talking! What a smart baby I have! I'm the happiest boy on earth!"

Dindi chattered happily too. They both ate until they couldn't hold any more. Boso chewed up tiny bits of meat and put them into Dindi's mouth until neither wanted any more. Then they snuggled together by their fire on their bed of ferns while the rain poured down on their wild-banana-leaf roof.

"This is the life for me," Boso said to Dindi the next day. "You and I both take to bush life just fine, don't we?"

They stayed several more days. Their sweet potatoes and sugar cane were gone but Dindi seemed content on water and the masticated food Boso fed him. Dindi learned to sit quietly while Boso hunted, then chatter happily with him as they rejoiced over their kill. He sucked contentedly on fatty drumsticks. Each night they played the '*Gi*' game, asking each other for things and giving them on cue, Dindi saying '*gi*' each time, whether he was giving or receiving it.

"It's time we start for home, Dindi," said Boso one day after a particularly good hunt. "Let's take this big wallaby and bush rat home to share with Ama. She'll be worrying about us if we don't go soon. And I'm hungry for sweet potato. These wild taro bulbs have been pretty good but I'd like some sweet potato and you must be thirsty for sugar juice."

Ama received her boys home happily. She enjoyed the meat, exclaiming sufficiently over it to satisfy the young hunter, and she listened with sincere interest to each tale of each hunt.

Boso and Dindi escaped to the bush again and again over the next several months. Dindi cut his first tooth on the drumstick of a cockatoo, and his second one on a piece of sugar cane. He learned to crawl around in the jungle foliage like a monkey. Finally he was toddling on his two feet. He seemed to love their times in the bush as much as Boso did. His little protein-starved body feasted on the fatty meat even before he had enough teeth to chew it.

Boso became an experienced hunter and trapper, and nobody rejoiced more over his kill than little Dindi. The brothers were absolutely inseparable, always talking to each other.

Boso made sure they were home on week-ends. He didn't want to miss the times when Apa and Tikira were home. Dindi never cried at night any more so the boys could sleep freely in the *tapanda*. They always did when the men were home from work on the bird-landing strip.

"Tsipoon! Tsipoon ni gi! (Give me the spoon,)" demanded the baby, holding out his little hand for the spoon Apa had brought from Kagua.

"Yes, yes. Pass the tsipoon to the child. He's going to take to white man's ways before the rest of us. Isn't that amazing how he always wants to eat with the tsipoon? Awkward sort of thing if you ask me. I could get used to using the thing though if I didn't mind the taste and the feel of the thing in my mouth! Who wants a big old hard thing in their mouth clattering around against their teeth?"

"My baby is almost out of babyhood. He has eight teeth now, Apa, and can eat everything we eat. He has sharp eyes and ears too. Two days ago he saw a wallaby in the bush before I did."

"It never ceases to amaze me how you have taught him to sit so quietly so you can hunt. What other child could learn so young?" pondered Apa.

"And what other child has learned to talk so young?" asked Kaisuwa. "That's the most surprising thing of all!"

"When we're all alone in the bush we talk to each other all the time, don't we, Dindi?"

"All the time, don't we?" answered Boso's little Echo.

The boys and men laughed heartily.

The baby looked around the fire at the happy faces and repeated, "all the time, don't we?"

"Speaking of learning to talk," said Apa when the laughter had died down, "how would you boys like to learn the white man's talk?"

"White man's talk?" repeated little Echo.

"Yes, Dindi, white man's talk."

"White man's talk."

"We would, Apa. We would like to learn the white man's talk," answered Boso. "How can we?"

"How can we?" echoed Dindi.

"Well, there's a chance we might get a man from the Tsimbu Tribe a long long ways away, to teach you. The turn-him-talk (*tainimtok*) at Kagua said if some villages are interested in their boys learning the white man's language and we're willing to feed and house the man, the *kapomani* (government) will pay him to come and teach our boys. I thought it might be a wise thing."

"I think it might be a wise thing, too, Apa," agreed Boso.

"Wise thing too, Apa," echoed Dindi.

"I don't know, boys," smiled Apa, looking at his two sons fondly.

"*Kapomani.* That word you just said. What does that mean? Is that another word for the white man?"

"No. Evidently there are two groups of white men. The *kapomani* (government) group are the ones who tell us to make the big wide barret roads and bird-landing strips. The other group are called mission."

"What do the *misini* do?"

"I'm not sure. I don't know what they do all the time, but I wanted to tell you what I saw one of them do, this work-time. I hardly know how to describe it. Someone said, 'One spirit is riding on the back of another spirit.' Somebody else said, 'One of those white men is riding on the back of one of his ancestors.' Someone else said he was riding on the back of a pig. But it was the biggest, strangest pig or ancestor or spirit I ever saw!"

"What did it look like, Apa? Please try to describe it."

"It ran like the wind and made a fearful clomping noise. It walked or ran on four legs like a pig, but that was its only similarity to a pig. It's back was nearly as high as my head ~ and its head ~ oh Brothers! It's head was longer than my forearm and hand together!"

The men and boys clicked their thumbnails off their front teeth.

"And its eyes! Oh, Brothers! Its eyes were absolutely huge!"

"And its mouth?"

"Yes, it has a mouth and teeth, and it crops the grass like a wallaby."

"Is it an overgrown wallaby, do you suppose?"

"Oh, no. It didn't look anything like a wallaby."

"Did it have hair?"

"Yes, it has hair like a cassowary tail on the top of its head and down the back of its long neck. Lovely hair! But loveliest of all was its tail. Its tail is all lovely long hair and it reaches clear to the ground!"

The men and boys snapped their thumbnails off their teeth in shocked unbelief. Dindi looked around at them with interest. He tried snapping his own little thumbnail off his own two little front teeth, but it didn't work. It didn't make any noise.

"And you should have seen that tail hair flying in the wind. It was like windblown bamboo tendrils, only so much more awesome because it was on a live creature. It was beautiful but terribly frightening! It ran so furiously! If it ran a man down it would be sure to kill him. He couldn't survive the tread of those four big feet that clattered against the stones like monstrous axes or something. I don't know what!"

"And a white man was riding on his back?"

"Yes. I know it sounds unbelievable," said Apa as they again clicked their thumbnails. "I would not have believed it if I had not seen it with my own eyes."

"He didn't fall off when it ran like the wind?"

"No, he didn't. Honestly he didn't. At first when it flashed by I thought it was all one creature with a man's head up from the middle of its back, and a monster head at the end of its neck, but later on I saw it standing by itself, eating grass, with no man on its back, and then I realized its actual shape."

"I'd like to go to Kagua with you to see this creature, Apa," said Boso.

"This creature, Apa," echoed Dindi.

"No, son, it wouldn't be safe. As I said, it could kill a man if it ran over him. I hate to think what it could do to a boy and a baby!"

So Boso had to wait several more years to see his first horse. '*Osi*' they called it. On her next visit home, Boso's sister told him one of her husband's relatives had seen the *osi* creature in Kagua and had come home and named his new son, '*Osi*.'

A few months later Tikira taught Boso the white man's word for sweet potato ~ *kaukau*. (pronounced cow-cow)

"*Kaukau*,"

"Can you count, Dindi?" asked Tikira.

"*Komea, lapo, repo, malapo*," immediately recited the little boy.

"Well, *komea* in their language is *one-fella*.

"*One-fella*."

"To say one sweet potato, you say *one-fella kaukau*."

(*wanpela kaukau*, pronounced *one-fella cow-cow*.)

"Two sweet potatoes is *two-fella kaukau*."

"*One-fella, two-fella, tree-fella, foa-fella*. That's the way you count *komea, laapo, repo, malapo*."

"*One-fella, two-fella, tree-fella, foa-fella*," repeated Boso.

"*One-fella, two-fella, tree-fella*, what?" asked Dindi.

"*Foa-fella*," said Tikira.

"*Foa-fella.*"

"*One-fella, two-fella, tree-fella, foa-fella,*" chanted the three brothers together.

CHAPTER EIGHT: LANGUAGE SCHOOL

"The Tsimbu teacher has come –yo –iyo-iyo."

The words were yodeled and "sung out" from one tribe to the next, from hill to valley, from one mountain to the next.

"The Tsimbu teacher has come. Everyone interested in learning the white man's language must gather at Sumbura."

"The Tsimbu teacher has come," Boso told Dindi. "Now we can learn the white man's language.

Tribe after tribe gathered together to meet the foreigner. They had never met anyone from the Tsimbu Province before.

"Is that he? That must be he! Oh-oh. He's a BIG man! And he doesn't look too friendly, does he, Dindi?"

"No," agreed Apa. "The Tsimbus aren't too friendly. The turn-him-talk said that before the white man came to our country the Tsimbus were the greatest fighters here. They were the ones who went farthest away to do battle. And they went on the longest trails to trade as well. They are a strong, courageous people. But they are no-

nonsense."

The Tsimbu could not speak their language. Consternation creased all faces as they listened to him babble. Their skin color was the same, but the sounds coming out of his mouth made no sense at all to them. At last a *turn-him-talk* came forward to translate his words to the crowd.

"The Tsimbu teacher says for each tribe to send three or four of your brightest boys to him." He stepped forward and grasped the arm of a boy in the crowd and pulled him to his feet.

"Choose boys of about this size; a little bigger or a little smaller would be all right, but not this size." He grabbed a younger boy and stood him in the center of the crowd.

"This one is too small. This one should stay at home with his mother. Don't send this size boy to the Tsimbu teacher."

Boso gave a long sigh of relief. He was the right size. He gave them his full attention as they specified time and place and told each tribe what food and how much firewood to bring the teacher.

"It's called 'school,'" said the turn-him-talk. "Send your brightest boys to school to learn the white man's ways and the white man's language.

"Boys, this is your chance of a lifetime. If you come to school and learn to speak the white man's language, you could very well be a turn-him-talk like me some day. The kapomani will give you free clothes like I'm wearing, free fish and rice, and all the money you want every fortnight to buy axes, knives, beads or shells or tobacco."

On the trail home that day, with Dindi riding on his shoulders, Boso hopped and skipped, bobbing Dindi up and down.

"I'm going to school, Dindi! I'm going to school!"

"I'm going to 'chool too?" asked Dindi.

"No, not you, my boy. You're too little. You can't go to school. You will have to sit outside real quietly and wait until I come out, just like when we go hunting. Okay?"

"Okay," agreed Dindi.

The first school morning Boso ran happily to Sumbura to the appointed house, Dindi bumping along on his shoulders. In his arms Boso carried two big sweet potatoes ~ the biggest Ama's garden could produce ~ a gift for his teacher.

"When I give them to him I will say 'cow-cow.' I'll surprise him with the white man's words I already know. One-fella, two-fella cow-cow, I'll say. Goody for me yo-iyo-iyo!"

"Goody for me-yo-iyo-iyo!" sang Dindi in his high little treble.

"Yes, goody for you as you sit real still outside the schoolhouse. You can lie down and have a nap when you want to, but you mustn't wander away. If you do, the big osi-creature might come and run right over you and eat you up. Chomp, chomp, chomp! Three bites and Dindi'd be gone! Will you stay close to the schoolhouse?"

"No more Dindi," said Dindi as he started to cry. "Dindi will stay close to the 'choolhouse!"

With a flourish, Boso swung the little boy from his shoulders to the ground, behind the house in which the boys were gathering.

"Stay here till I come back," he admonished and was gone.

Hours later when Boso came out to collect his charge all his exuberance seem to have faded. He trudged home in silence. Dindi, too, kept silent on his shoulders.

"How was school?" asked Ama.

"Terrible!"

"Terrible? How was it terrible?"

"He tells us to say so much at once and we can't remember it all. Most of the time we haven't any idea what he means, or what he's telling us to do. He yells at us. He twists our ears when we don't say it right. I don't even know what I am saying. How can I know if it is right or wrong?"

"Wasn't the turn-him-talk there to explain it to you?"

"No, there wasn't any turn-him-talk anywhere around. I wish I didn't have to go back tomorrow."

"Oh, come on, now. Surely it can't be that bad."

"Yes, it is bad. If I didn't want to learn the white man's language so much I wouldn't go back for one more single day!"

"See if you can't find courage and strength to bear it until the week-time-end when Apa comes home. You can tell him all about it then. He would be terribly disappointed in you for giving up because of a little hardship. Now, wouldn't he?"

"Yes, I suppose you're right."

"Of course, I'm right. Apa thinks it is very important to learn to talk with the white man!"

"I know. And I thought it was important too. I just didn't suppose it would be so hard."

"Anything that is really important is hard to get, usually. The white man's axes are important to us, and they are hard to get. Winning a battle over our enemies is important to us, and that's not easy either."

"That's true."

"Look at this white man's language as though it were your battle. Let's see if you can't be the victor! The hero!"

The three sat in silence around the fire. Dindi had been listening carefully, turning his face from one to the other as they spoke. He was growing up a little more mentally, than physically, and learning not to interrupt. But now in the silence he asked, "Boso not happy?"

"No, Dindi, I'm not happy."

"No more goody for 'chool?"

"Right. I don't feel like saying goody for school anymore."

"Did you say cow-cow?"

"No, I didn't even get to say one-fella cow-cow, two-fella cow-cow."

"Why not?" asked Ama.

"Why not?" asked Dindi.

"When I went into the schoolhouse I saw the boys were putting the sweet potatoes in a pile by the door, but mine were so big I wanted to show them to him and make my little surprise speech. But he saw me coming to him and he pointed to the pile and said something I couldn't understand. He seemed so stern and unfriendly that I gave up and just went and put my *kaukau* with the other boys'."

"So the day began with a disappointment," soothed Ama.

"And then went from bad to worse," moaned Boso.

"From bad to worse," echoed Dindi.

"Did he twist your ears?" asked Ama.

"Did he twist your ears?" asked Dindi.

"No, not yet. But he will tomorrow. I just know he will."

"Maybe it won't be so bad tomorrow," suggested Ama. But it was.

"Did he twist your ears?" Dindi learned to ask on the way home each afternoon.

"Yes, he twisted them two times today. They still hurt."

"Poor Boso. My poor Boso," said Dindi, patting Boso's shoulder as he spoke.

Franday afternoon when Boso lifted Dindi to his shoulders, he said, "Let's hurry home. Apa will be home tonight. We can tell him all about it. Don't touch my right ear, Dindi. It hurts. See, it's been bleeding."

"It's been bleeding," echoed Dindi in consternation as he observed the wounded ear and dried blood from his vantage point right by the ear. "My poor Boso!"

"Let's go first to Ama's house. I'm hungry," said Boso as they neared Kati-loma.

"I'm hungry too."

Ama already had some sweet potatoes cooked for her hungry boys.'

"How was school today," she asked.

"Terrible! He twisted my ear so hard two times today he made it bleed."

"He made it bleed?" Ama was shocked. "Why, the rascal!" She clicked her thumbnail against her teeth as she looked at the dried blood on Boso's ear.

"Why, the rascal," echoed Dindi, and he tried to click his thumbnail. He finally got it to click.

"I did it, Boso! Listen!"

"Yes, you did," laughed Boso in spite of himself and his troubles.

"You're properly sympathetic, Dindi. Good for you," laughed Ama.

As soon as both boys filled their tummies Boso said, "Well, Ama, we're going to the *tapanda* to wait for Apa. We'll see you there later when you bring Apa his sweet potatoes."

"Okay, *pulupape, nana naki lapo.*"

Boso told Kaisuwa all about his trials at school as they sat around the fire waiting for Apa's arrival. Kaisuwa too, was properly sympathetic.

Before long they heard the yodeling song of the approaching work crew. Dindi climbed on Boso's shoulders, as Boso lit the pitpit torch in the fire.

"Let's go! Let's go!" he urged.

"Here we go. Ouch! Watch my ear!"

"Sorry, Boso, sorry!"

They hurried up the trail with others who were coming to greet the returning crew. When they reached them, they fell in behind, joining the yodeling chorus.

"We've been to work in Kagua-yo –iyo –iyo –iyo.

"We've been to see the white man's world-iyo –iyo – iyo.

"We've worked so hard leveling the land-iyo –iyo – iyo.

"We've dug up rocks and carried them away-iyo-iyo-iyo

"We've chopped down trees and burned the brush-iyo-iyo-iyo

"We've made a place for the Big Bird to land-iyo-iyo-iyo

"Some day we'll bring home the white man's axes-iyo-iyo-iyo

"And the white man's knives! –iyo-iyo-iyo."

"And how are my sons?" asked Apa, laying his big hands on both Boso's and Dindi's knees at the same time, after he had eaten an unbelievable number of sweet potatoes.

"Boso's ear's been bleeding," announced Dindi.

"St-st, so it has! Were you a numbskull at school?" asked Apa.

"How did you know?" asked Boso in surprise.

"I've stood beside the school at Kagua and watched the Tsimbu teacher there try to teach those boys. When no one can give him the right answers, he twists some ears."

"But it's hard! It's hard, Apa, to learn a new language!"

"Oh, no, not for a young boy like you, surely! For a mature man like me, yes. My ears have hardened. They can't hear new sounds. But your ears ought to be soft and receptive yet."

"But he gets so mad and yells so loud I can't think!"

"Remember how you've been told men yell in battle? You'll never make a good warrior if you can't concentrate midst yelling."

"But it hurts so badly when he twists my ears!"

"No worse than a battle wound, now, surely?"

Boso hung his head.

"You can't tell me it hurts worse than a battle wound? Come on, Son, put a stone in your liver and go with courage to meet this new challenge."

"But you've never spilled my blood, Apa, like some fathers do their sons', so I didn't think you'd let this Tsimbu man spill it either."

"Ah, maybe I haven't trained a very good warrior?

Maybe I have raised a lily-livered son, eh?"

"No, Apa! No!"

"Well, don't let me hear any complaints then. If he twists your ear clear off, I might listen. Did you hear me complaining when they nearly cut my arm and shoulder off?"

"No, Apa."

"Well, then. What did I do?"

"You bound it back on with vines and healing leaves and crawled home."

"Would you like me to bind up your ear with vines and leaves?"

"No, Apa. It's nothing. Nevermind." Boso was glad Dindi had mentioned it first.

"Hey, that sounds like someone I recognize now! That sounds like my Son!"

Boso grinned.

"Do you pay attention to the Tsimbu teacher, Son? Do you listen closely with both ears?"

"Yes, Apa."

"Okay, then. Just make sure you never let yourself chatter with the boys. There will be plenty of time for your boyish chatter when the teacher goes back to the Tsimbu, but there won't be any other way then to gain the white man's wisdom."

"Are they wise, Apa?"

"Exceedingly wise, my Son. Great wisdom enables them to control the flight of the biggest birds man has ever seen. To call them out of the skies, then to send them back up again, carrying man, can you imagine it?

"Great wisdom enables them to tame and ride the huge 'osi creature, five or six times bigger, maybe ten times bigger than themselves.

"Great wisdom alone enables them to get fish in tsin cans and sharp steel axes from the spirit world or wherever they get them. Either it is great wisdom or great magic. Whichever it is we need to learn it.

"Great wisdom or magic enables them to decrease the size of a man and put him in a small box that you can carry around in your hands and listen to him talk or sing."

"Really, Apa, or is it just a fairy tale?"

"It sounds like a fairy tale, doesn't it? Like the one where the big woman decreases the man to a size small enough to fit into her net head covering?"

"Yes, that's the one I thought of. You're not telling me the white man really does that? You didn't see him do it, did you?"

"No, I didn't see him do it with my own eyes. It's only what I heard. Let me tell you about it."

Boso and Dindi settled themselves more comfortably, ready for a story.

"There was a man on our work-crew at the bird-landing strip who speaks our language, although he pronounces some words differently. He comes from a village between Kagua and Ialibu. He said many, many moons ago his youngest son left home to go to the white man's world. He was gone so long the man supposed the white man had eaten him long since. But he came back a couple moons ago, bigger and stronger and healthier. He laughed at his father's fears. He said white men don't eat people. He said they don't allow anyone else to eat people either. If they catch anyone eating human flesh they put them in the calaboose, he said."

"What's a calaboose?"

"I don't know for sure. All I know is that it's a place you can't get out of until they let you. If we don't work fast enough, the policeman asks us if we want to go to the calaboose.

"Anyway, this man's son brought him a gift."

"What was it?"

"It was called a wireless in the white man's language, but who knows what that means. The man's son said it was just a name, he guessed, because he couldn't translate the word into our language. Anyway, it was a small black box with little protrusions and marks on it. If you turned these protrusions or knots or whatever they were, you could hear a man talking from inside the box."

Boso and Kaisuwa and everyone else clicked their thumbnails off their teeth, and Dindi hurried to do the same.

"He really talked?" asked Kaisuwa. "Your friend could hear him?"

"Yes. He said he heard him very well, many times."

"What did the man-in-the-box say?"

"I don't know. My friend couldn't understand him. He didn't speak our language. But he talked and talked for days. It seemed he could talk all day and half the night without tiring. Sometimes he sang songs. Sometimes he played beautiful music. My friend said it was lovelier music than you could make on a Jews-harp or a bamboo flute or a kundu drum. He said they must have some other kind of thing they make music on."

"Does he still have this man-in-the-box?"

"Well, he still has the box, but he thinks the man died."

"Died?" Velar clicks in the throats. "How did he die?"

"He didn't eat. He must have starved to death. Every night my friend put out sweet potatoes for him but he didn't eat them. My friend then tried bananas and sugar cane and mushrooms and everything else he could think of, but he guessed the man didn't like them because every morning the food was still there, untouched. The man-in-the-box's voice just got weaker and weaker. My friend pled with him to eat. He told him he didn't have any tsin fish or *kusa* or any other white man's food. He begged the little man-in-the-box to just try ours ~ just take a few nibbles. But he never did and he died."

"Maybe he couldn't get out of the box. Maybe that is the *calaboose*?"

"Yes, I suggested that, though I did not connect it with the word, calaboose. I told him he should have tried to open the box to help the man out. And he said he did try.

He tried very hard to open the box, but he was not able. The only thing left to try, he said, was to smash it on rocks, but he didn't think of that until the man had been dead for some days, so there was no use destroying his interesting little box, he said. People might not believe his story if he didn't have the box to prove it."

"But there had to have been an opening in the box somewhere for the white man to have put the man inside."

"I know, unless he sealed it by magic. My friend hoped the man-in-the-box knew the magic to open it and come out, but evidently he didn't know the magic, or else he didn't like our food, so he died."

"What did the man's son say who had brought him the gift?"

"His son doesn't know the man died. He had to go back to his work. He was only able to stay two days with his father. He said it had taken him three days to walk from a place called Hagen, and he only had one week-time off work."

"Was there any odor of decaying flesh from the box?" asked Kaisuwa.

"No. Someone asked him that and he said there wasn't."

"How does he account for that?"

"He figures it is all part of the white man's magic."

"Oh, of course."

"Did he know if the man in the box was another white man, or a black man like us?"

"He doesn't know. It could have been a policeman from the coast or a Tsimbu or a white man, he says. He couldn't recognize any of these languages at that time, he says. He wishes he had a chance at it now again, since he has heard the white man, and the policemen and the Tsimbus. But the man-in-the-box is dead now, so there is no hope of ever hearing his voice again to try to analyze it with the new knowledge gained form our recent experiences and exposure to these other men."

"Apa, do you suppose the wireless is another name for the calaboose where they put people who eat human flesh?"

"I don't know, my Son. There's so much I don't know. There's so much to learn. That's why you need to go to school and learn their language."

"Yes, we must learn to understand them if they have magic like this! Why, we might get put in a box just for doing something we didn't even know would displease them!"

Boso and Dindi enjoyed Sararay and Sunday immensely. They spent the whole time with Apa and Tikira.

"When will I be big enough to go to Kagua with you, Apa?"

"Not for a while yet, Son. Go to school and learn the white man's language. Remember, they yell at us in there at Kagua too. They don't twist our ears but some of those policemen really do push and slap men around. It's not all that much fun sometimes. Go to school and keep both ears wide open and your mouth shut, unless the Tsimbu tells you to speak."

Fortunately it was easier the second week-time. Somehow Boso managed the right response to one of the Tsimbu teacher's questions the fourth day of that school week, Fonday. He went out to collect his baby in the best spirits he had exhibited since school had started.

"Do you want to bounce on my shoulders?" asked Boso.

"I want to bounce on your shoulders," replied Dindi. They bounced and chattered along the trail.

"*Me-fella kaikai kaukau,*" said Dindi.

Boso stopped. He stood stock still in shock.

"What did you say?"

"*Me-fella kaikai kaukau.*"

Boso slipped Dindi from his shoulders and held him in front of him, face to face.

"Say it again."

"*Me-fella kaikai cow-cow.*"

"*Me-fella kaikai kaukau,*" repeated Boso. "Do you know what that means?"

"No."

"It means, 'we are eating sweet potatoes.'"

"It means, 'we are eating sweet potatoes,'" echoed Dindi.

"What else can you say that you heard while you were sitting outside the school?"

Dindi looked thoughtful.

"*Me-fella ologeta sin-down.*"

"*Me-fella ologeta sin-down,*" echoed Boso. "How can you remember them, Dindi? I can repeat them after the Tsimbu but there are so many of them I forget them as soon as I've said them. Say it again."

"*Me-fella ologeta sin-down.*"

"*Me-fella ologeta sin-down,*" echoed Boso again. "That means we are all sitting down together, or all of us are sitting down." The Tsimbu makes us sit down while we are saying it. Then he makes us stand up and he says, '*Me-fella ologeta tsan-up.*'"

"*Me-fella ologeta tsan-up,*" echoed Dindi.

"Oh, Dindi, this is wonderful! You're going to learn Talk Pidgin before I do! Let's go home and see if you can say them to Ama."

They hurried on their way now, chatting those three Pidgin sentences to each other. Then Dindi remembered another word. '*Pickaninny! Pickaninny! Ologeta yu-fella pickaninny sin-down.*"

"That's right! *Pickaninny*! That means *nokonaki* ~ children! *Ologeta yu-fella pikinini sindaun* means all of you children sit down."

"Oh, Dindi, this is wonderful! I can't believe it! You're just a baby! How can you talk the white man's talk?"

"I'm not a baby. I'm a big boy!"

"Yes, you are! You sure are a big boy!"

Ama too was delighted. She listened happily to her boys chatting their Pidgin sentences back and forth to each other all evening.

"I will just have to let the Tsimbu know that you can speak Talk Pidgin, Dindi, but how will I do it? How can I say my baby can talk Pidgin?. I don't know how to say baby in Pidgin."

"I'm not a baby!"

"Okay, you're not a baby. Then you're a *pickaninny.* I'll tell him '*Pikinini talk Pidgin*' and maybe he will understand. I don't even know how to say little, so I could say 'little *pikinini*.'"

Boso sat Dindi just outside the schoolhouse door the next morning. He put a stone in his liver and went straight to his teacher.

"*Pikinini tok Pisin,*"

"*Who's 'at?*" asked the teacher.

Boso pointed to the door and said, "*Pickanini talk Pidgin,*" once again.

"*You go kiss-him,*" said the teacher.

Boso looked at him blankly.

The teacher gave Boso a little push in the direction of the door and repeated, "*You go kiss-him.*"

Boso started toward the door, then realized his teacher was following him. Once outside he picked up Dindi and held him there at the door.

"*Who's 'at pickaninny? Him baby-ya! Pickaninny talk-him Pidgin, a? You talk-him! Me like hear-him. You talk-him,*" said the teacher.

"*La, Dindi! Pidgin la!*" urged Boso.

"*Me-fella kaikai kaukau,*" said the baby voice.

"*All-the-man!*" yelled the Tsimbu. "*You-fella kaikai kaukau-ya? Good-fella! Good-fella true!*"

"*Menda la!*" urged Boso. (Say another one.)

"*Pickaninny ologeta sin-down,*" said Dindi.

"*All-the-man! Pickaninny ologeta sin-down ya? You come long me. You pickaninny, you baby, you come long me. You come sin-*

down long table belong me! Come!" He held out his hands to Dindi.

Boso handed Dindi to the teacher and Dindi allowed himself to be taken and lifted in the burley Tsimbu's arms.

"*You good-fella baby! You number one monkey!*" said the teacher.

Dindi well understood that he was being praised even though he had never heard those words before. He looked at Boso and said, "*You number one monkey.*"

Boso laughed. "*You number one monkey,*" he echoed, pointing his finger at Dindi.

Dindi pointed his tiny index finger back at Boso, "*You number one monkey!*"

"*Hey, you two-fella! You two-fella no can talk fight. Fasten mouth,*" commanded the Tsimbu.

"*Fasten mouse,*" echoed Dindi to the best of his ability.

The burley Tsimbu laughed a big burley laugh. He cupped one hand over his mouth and repeated, "*Fasten mouth!*"

Dindi cupped his little hand over his mouth and said, "*Fasten mouse.*" Turning to Boso, he repeated, "*Fasten mouse, Boso.*"

Boso covered his mouth and said, "*Fasten mouse, Dindi.*"

The teacher laughed and set Dindi down on the big crate which served for his desk.

"Talk-him ologeta pikininny," he said waving his arm at the children.

"Ologeta pikinini," yelled Dindi, "Fasten mouse."

The crowd of children covered their mouths as Dindi did.

"Behind-him him," commanded the teacher. (Repeat after him.)

The children all looked blankly at the teacher, not understanding.

"*This-fella pikinini savvy talk Pidgin. You-fella behind-him him.*"

Again there was a pause.

"Pidgin la!" Boso commanded Dindi. (Speak Pidgin.) *"Me-fella kaikai kaukau."*

"Behind-him him," said the teacher pointing to the baby. He made motion of eating, saying, *"Me-fella kaikai kaukau."*

Boso and Dindi repeated, *"Me-fella kaikai kaukau."*

All the boys repeated, *"Me-fella kaikai kaukau."*

"Good-fella! Good-fella! This-fella baby good-fella teacher!"

"This-fella baby good-fella teacher," said Boso, delighted to have his teacher so happy.

The teacher tapped Dindi's bare chest, *"Talk-him all pickininny, me good-fella monkey."*

Dindi tapped his own chest saying, *"Me good-fella monkey."* (I'm a good boy.)

All the boys tapped their own chests and echoed, *"Me good-fella monkey."*

The morning passed quickly as the baby echoed everything the teacher said, causing the normally stern teacher to laugh so hard he sometimes held his sides, or wiped the tears from his eyes. The boys echoed Dindi's words and seemed to learn more in one morning than they had learned in the whole previous two weeks.

At noon the Tsimbu sent the boys out to play, but he kept Dindi and Boso with him. He fed them tinned fish and rice. Dindi smacked his little lips and said, "Good-fella fis!" in answer to the teacher's questions. When his tummy was full he lay down on the teacher's crate and went to sleep. He had had a full morning.

When classes resumed the big Tsimbu spoke softly. "Sh-sh. *Baby sleep. Talk easy-easy."* (Speak softly.)

"Sh-sh. *Baby sleep. Talk easy-easy,"* repeated Boso.

All the boys repeated, "Sh-sh. *Baby sleep. Talk easy-easy."*

When Dindi wakened later he was in high good humor, crowing happy laughter and repeating long intricate Pidgin sentences. Boso absolutely could not believe his ears. Where his tongue floundered Dindi seemed to have no difficulty whatsoever. At the end of a long delightful day the teacher admonished Boso, "*Kiss-him baby he come next Monday.*" (Bring the baby next Monday.)

"*Monday baby come?*" Boso asked, wanting to make sure he heard correctly.

"Yes! Yes! Kiss-him baby he come next Monday!"

"Yes! Yes! Kiss-him baby he come next Monday," echoed Dindi.

Nodding his head vigorously as the teacher was doing, Boso said, "Yes! Yes!"

"Yes, yes!" echoed Dindi, nodding his head.

Boso took Dindi from the teacher's arms and they hurried home to tell Ama.

"Nobody got their ears pulled or twisted once today, Ama! Dindi talked so well and so cute that he made the teacher laugh and we all laughed and learned better than ever before!"

When they were finally seated by the fire with Apa that night in the tapanda and he said, "Well, Boso, how is school going?" Dindi answered first. "Nobody got their ears pulled once today, Apa."

"Oh, really now, Dindi. How do you know anything about school?"

"I went to 'chool today," answered the toddler proudly.

"Aw, come now. Surely not! They don't take babies!"

"I'm not a baby. *Me good-fella monkey,*" said Dindi, tapping his chest and lapsing into Pidgin.

"What's this?"

"Yes, Apa," put in Boso. "You must hear him! Dindi can talk Pidgin better than any of us school boys. The teacher had me bring him into class today and we had a wonderful time." He told Apa the story of their whole exciting day.

"*La, Dindi, Pidgin la!* Let Apa hear some of the things you can say."

"*Ologeta pickininny, fasten mouse,*" said Dindi clapping one little hand over his mouth. Boso repeated it in Pidgin, and then interpreted it for his father. They went on for half an hour, jogging each other's memories and repeating all they knew, with Boso translating when he could.

"Well, I'm delighted. Absolutely delighted!" announced Apa when they had exhausted their repertoire. " You make my liver quiver! You swell my liver with happiness! What a lucky man I am! I sent one son off to school to learn the white man's language and here I have two sons spouting white man's words like a bubbling spring! Ah, we shall learn the white man's ways and the white man's wisdom too. With two sons like mine, who can hold the Kati-loma down? Whether it be battles or words or secret wisdom, we shall overcome! We shall win, Dindi and Boso! We shall win the day!"

CHAPTER NINE: A STEEL AXE AND A WHITE MAN

"*You me two-fella go look-him Papa*," said Dindi one *Franday* night a month later.

"Okay, we'll go see Apa," agreed Boso picking up the pitpit torch.

"Come on, *liklik monkey*, climb up on my shoulders," he continued, for he had now learned the Pidgin word for little. *Liklik monkey* means little boy.

"*Papa! Papa belong me!*" called Dindi as the men approached and before Boso had even located his father in the crowd of men.

"My son, come to me," answered Apa. "Come and see what I have to show you."

"An axe! The white man's axe!" squealed Boso. "Oh, Apa, may I hold it? May I carry it?"

"Here, give me Dindi first. He might get cut if you try to carry both him and the axe. It's sharper than anything you have ever seen in your life before."

Apa lifted Dindi from Boso's shoulders and put him on his own.

"Whee!" squealed Dindi. "Now I can see the whole

world!" He seldom got to ride so high.

Apa pulled the white man's axe from his bark belt where he had been carrying it as he always carried his stone axe. He handed it to Boso.

"All-the-man! It's heavy, isn't it?"

"Yes, it is such a big steel head, you see. They must have the root of steel that they could lavish so much on one steel axe-head!"

"There is to be no more fighting, Son."

"No more fighting, Apa? Never?"

"'Never any more,' the white man says. If we fight he will put us in the calaboose."

"No more battles? Oh, Apa, you mean I'll never get to be a great warrior like you? Oh, Apa, is this the end of the world?"

"No, not quite, Son. We must go on. There's a lot to be learning and a lot to be doing. But we've got a lot done. We have one end of the bird-landing strip completed, and a bird came and landed at Kagua three days ago."

"Really, Apa? You've seen the big bird on the ground?"

"Yes, I have, and wait until I tell you. It's not a real live bird at all."

"It's not a real live bird? Then how does it fly?"

"That, my Son, is the big question. How does it fly? It has wings like a bird, but it is not a bird. It's hard. Almost as hard as this steel axe, though not as heavy, of course. It has no soft feathers."

"How big was it?"

"It was bigger than your Ama's house but the white man said it is just a small bird. He said the bigger birds will come when we lengthen the landing strip."

At Mambore, they lit their pitpit torch at a *tapanda* fire.

Most of the men continued on toward Sumbura, Ronga and Batri. Mambi and the Sakamapi and Wakipanda men turned south toward Katiloma.

Boso carried Apa's axe all the way home. Dindi rode high on Apa's shoulders, occasionally fingering Apa's bigwig softly.

Once they reached home they examined the steel axe carefully by the fire. What a treasure! Each one took a turn holding it and caressing it. Boso even laid his lips against its coolness. Dindi, of course, did the same.

"I have something else to show you," said Apa.

"It couldn't be as wonderful as this steel axe, surely?"

"No, Boso, it isn't that wonderful, and it isn't even ours. But it's something we need to consider and discuss.

Apa sucked in his stomach and reached into the front of his bark belt. He pulled out a small square packet wrapped carefully in bark covering and tied with woven bark string. He untied the string and unwrapped a photograph of a man.

"Of all the spirits!" exclaimed Kaisuwa as he jumped back in horror.

"Somebody captured that man's spirit!" exclaimed Naki-Pa.

"Yes. They did that all right," agreed Mambi.

"Who did it, Apa?" asked Boso.

"The white man."

"And is the purpose of it black magic?" asked Kaisuwa.

"My friend says no. This is his son who went out to work on a coffee plantation. He's the one who brought his father the black magic box called a wireless.

"My friend asked his son why he allowed the white men to capture his spirit in this way. His answer was because they wouldn't do him any harm. My friend told him he was extremely foolish. If sorcery can kill a man with just a captured hair, or fingernail paring, or a bit of feces, what torturous death could they make a man die when they have his whole spirit?

"Well, the son says white men never use sorcery. He said they put people who practice witchcraft and black magic in the calaboose. My friend told him even if his master didn't make use of witchcraft some other white man might, and so he was extremely foolish to let his spirit be captured in this way.

"He then said, 'Okay, I'll leave it with you, my Apa, and you can see to it that it doesn't fall into my enemies' hands.' My friend has often thought he ought to burn it but he's not even sure that burning it might not cause his son harm or perhaps death. Could a man live if his spirit were burned? Anyway he says it is pleasant to look at his son's face in his absence, so he hasn't destroyed it yet. He brought it to me, asking my advice."

"He's a good looking man," observed Boso.

"What will your advice be, my Son?" asked Kaisuwa.

"I'll have to think on it until Monday. I'll take it back to him then."

They sat in silence, staring into the fire, thinking of all the strange phenomena that went with the white man's world, until Dindi's small voice brought them back to their own.

"Apa, I want a bark belt."

"Ah, you're too little for a bark belt, Dindi. You're hardly more than a baby yet. Wait until you grow tall and lose your first baby tooth. Then I'll make you a bark belt."

"No. I don't want to wait. I'm not a baby. I'm a big boy now. I go to school every day. I'm the only boy at school with no *bilum* and *tanket* leaves. Ama will make me a string to hold some leaves, she says, but I want a bark belt like you and Boso."

"Bark belts are uncomfortable, Son. In order to keep them from sliding down, we have to sew them on very tightly. That will crowd your big tummy and make you have to throw your shoulders way back to make room for it. That's good discipline for boys. It makes them walk like a man, but you're too young to have to endure that yet."

Dindi jumped to his feet. He sucked his tummy in and threw his shoulders back and strutted around the men and boys.

"I can do it, Apa. I can do it! I'm your big grown-up *ere pere naki*. Let me have a bark belt." (Last son.)

"Nevermind for the moment. I'll think on it," replied Apa.

The next morning when Dindi had slipped out alone to the bad place, Boso heard his father ask his grandfather, "What do you say, Kaisuwa? Isn't Dindi too young for a bark belt?"

"Maybe not. He's so mature in his thinking. He may be truly ashamed of his nakedness. I've been working on a narrow belt for him here, in case you give your approval."

"Oh. He has asked about this before last night?"

"Yes, he's been pestering Boso about it for days. Boso told him he could ask you when you came."

"I see. It's not a sudden impulse he will have forgotten by now, then. Let's see the belt."

When Dindi returned he gladly laid across Apa's lap while Apa sewed it in place. Apa then drew a new red laplap from his shoulder billum. With his sharp steel axe he cut a nick in it. He tore one-third of it from the remainder, folded it several times, then draped it from the front of the bark belt.

Dindi danced a little jig.

"Oh, Apa, I like it! I like it!"

They laughed at the happy little boy who looked so cute in his new belt and drape.

"Come, Dindi," said Boso. "Let's go get you some tanket leaves to cover your bottom, and then you will be fully dressed."

"Just wait, Boso," said Apa. "My other son, the school boy, ought to have the rest of this red laplap for his front covering."

Boso stood quietly in front of his father while he folded and draped the laplap from his belt, over the top of the old string net covering. The new cloth felt soft against his stomach, groin and legs. Boso felt loved and cherished, just like he had the times his father rubbed his body with melted lard and decorated his hair with feathers for the *singsing* dance.

When Apa was done, Boso took both his father's hands in his own, and pressed them to his stomach.

"Apa, you swell my liver with happiness. You make my liver quiver! I like this new red tapa. I will be so proud to go to school in it Monday, and to take Dindi in his."

"I'm proud of my sons and how well you are both learning the white man's language."

"Boso! Boso! Don't we look nice?"

Dindi danced a childish imitation of the *singsing* dance.

"Yo! Yo! Here I come in my new tapa-yo! –iyo!"

"Come on, monkey, let's go get your *tanket* leaves."

Dindi grasped Boso's hand and hopped and danced beside him off the porch.

That night Dindi squirmed and wriggled, unable to sleep in his tight bark belt.

"What's the matter, Dindi?"

"I can't sleep."

"Why not?"

"I'm too full, I guess."

"Oh, your belt is too tight."

Dindi didn't answer and Boso dozed off only to be reawakened by the still wriggling little form.

"Do you want me to cut it off?"

"No," whimpered Dindi.

As Boso was dropping off again, Dindi asked, "Apa wouldn't sew it back on again, if you cut it off, would he?"

"No. Not for many moons, he wouldn't."

Dindi finally fell asleep and Boso let him sleep late the next morning. The little boy learned to eat less at night, until he grew accustomed to the tight bark band around his middle.

The boys had a great week in school, and Mambi had a good week in Kagua, working with his new axe. They gathered around the fire again the following Franday night.

"Guess what? I don't go to work in Kagua on Monday."

"Is the landing strip done, Apa?" asked Boso.

"No, but something very exciting is going to happen."

"Tell us quick," urged Dindi.

"The white man is going to come out here."

"Here to Katiloma?"

"Well, near here. He will come to Sumbura."

"Why?"

"He is coming to take a census. 'Kiss-him name' they call it in Pidgin."

"We have to give them our names?" asked Kaisuwa.

"Yes."

"What will he do with them?"

"He will write them down on paper."

"For purposes of witchcraft?"

"No. For counting. White men are always counting, it seems. Counting time. Counting days. Counting men at work. Counting their steps down the bird-landing strip, counting the weight of sweet potatoes, bananas and everything! I guess they just like to count."

"So do I," put in Dindi. "One-fella, two-fella, tree-fella."

"Yes, my last son. You are growing up half old-world and half new-world. You will help us all to make the necessary changes and adjustments."

"I wonder if the teacher will call off school," pondered Boso. "I would like to go see this white man."

"Oh, most definitely. Everyone has to be there, old and young, male and female."

"Even babies and old women?" asked Boso.

"Yes. Everyone who is alive. We aren't allowed to leave out anyone."

"But not the babies who don't have names yet?"

"Even them."

"But how can he take their names if they don't have names?"

"He wants to see them, even if they haven't been named."

"Do people give him their real names?" asked Kaisuwa.

"You don't have to. Some people make up names and give them to him, I heard. It's okay, I guess, as long as you remember to answer to that name at the next census."

"He will come back and do it all over again later?"

"Yes, again and again. Then he will know who has died and who has been born. And we have to tell him how each person died."

"What if we don't know. What if we aren't sure who poisoned each one, or who used black magic on them?"

"I don't know. We just tell him what we think, I guess."

Boso thought he had never seen as big of a crowd as gathered at Sumbura for the census. Tribe by tribe and family by family, his people stood before the strange white man as they gave him their names.

Boso lost his fear of the bristle-handed, toeless creature as he sat under the brush arbor calling out questions in Pidgin. Boso could see at once that the creature's feet were encased in some sort of wrapping. That's why we can't see the prints of his toes when he walks, he thought. He is a man as my father is a man. How can they doubt it simply because he is a bird of a different species? He differs from us as the cockatoo differs from the bird of paradise, but both are birds. Our men are the finer feathered birds in their fur-trimmed *singsing* billums and new greased *tanket* leaves. However the khaki tapa fitting the white man's form so closely, is interesting too.

Boso stood near his father with Dindi's hand in his, in line with his father's four wives and other children, when their turn came. It was almost big-sun by this time.

"And what is the baby's name?" asked the white man when he came to Dindi.

Dindi didn't wait for the turn-him-talk to translate. He spoke up himself.

"Name belong me Dindi. Me no baby. Me big-fella monkey," he answered, stretching himself to his tallest limit.

"Ho, ho," laughed the white man. "You no baby? You big-fella monkey? Who's-'at learn-him this-fella big-fella monkey long talk Pidgin?"

"Tsimbu teacher learn-him me time me go long school," answered Dindi.

"You go long school?" asked the white man. "All-he no savvy kiss-him baby long school."

"All-he kiss-him me. Me no baby."

"All right. All right. Come." The white man held out his arms toward Dindi. "Come talk-him me 'gain."

Dindi went toward him, pulling Boso by the hand to accompany him.

"Which of your father's wives is the mother of this baby boy?" the turn-him-talk asked Boso.

"None of these," answered Boso. "His mother died when he was small. I take care of him now."

Boso listened as the turn-him-talk translated his words for the white man. Dindi allowed himself to be lifted in the white man's arms and sat upon his knee. Standing right beside the man, Boso drew in deep breaths. How differently the white man smelled. There were strange odors. He couldn't label them.

"Stay here by me," said this strange smelling man. "I have never met a bush-pickaninny this small who could talk to me in Pidgin like this. Stay here and when I have finished the Kati-loma tribe names we'll have a bit to eat while we chat together."

Dindi sat perfectly still on the white man's knee and watched carefully as he wrote each name down in his book. When the tribe's names and relationships were all recorded the white man stood with Dindi in his arms and walked into a small hut built for his visit. Boso followed closely.

"How about some fish and rice?" the man suggested.

"Thank you," answered Dindi. "Me two-fella like-him fis-n-lice."

"You two-fella like-him fis-n-lice, eh?" And the man

119

laughed loud and long. Boso smiled and warmed to this man with the big booming laugh. Dindi laughed too, to hear the man laugh.

The boys enjoyed watching every action of this man and his cook. They were introduced to bread and tinned meat and found them both appealing.

When they were done eating, Dindi slipped off the man's lap and put both hands on one of his high-top shoes.

"What is it?" he asked.

"My shoe. It's my shoe."

"Shoe," repeated Dindi, looking at Boso. "Shoe."

"My people thought the shoes were part of his legs. They thought he had toeless feet," Boso said to the turn-him-talk."

The turn-him-talk translated, and the white man laughed his big, booming laugh again.

"Ah, yes, a popular misconception. Like the old German killed and eaten on the coast last century. They boiled his boots for days and said they never did get tender. Yes, they thought they were a part of him."

The turn-him-talk translated all this for Boso. They prepared to return to the census.

"Why don't you go down to Ronga with me tomorrow? I'd like your company. Would your father let you?" the white man asked the boys.

Apa gave his consent and so it came about that Boso and Dindi accompanied the first white man on his first census to Puri, Ronga and Batri. Their Pidgin vocabulary grew by leaps and bounds in those days. They even learned many English words.

The white man came to the end of his census reluctantly.

"I haven't been so well entertained in years! I will never forget this census!"

"Me too me like-him," responded Dindi, and Boso echoed his brother's assertion. "I enjoyed it too!"

They walked back to Sumbura together and said their good-byes in sight of Mambi and other members of the family as well as many onlookers.

"You have two great sons there, Mambi," said the white man. "I would like to take them back to Kagua with me, but I know I must return them to you. You are their father. I hope I am chosen to do the next census here, so I may see them again."

"I am sure they will be delighted to see you again," returned Mambi, hugging his boys to him.

"Those heads are full of brains," said the white man, tousling their hair. "I would like to see them get the kind of education we give our children in our world. But Papua, and New Guinea have a ways to go before that is realistic. I return them to your care. May they be well and happy. Thank you for letting them go walkabout with me."

"Thank you for bringing them back safely to me. I am sure they had a good time."

"Good-bye," said the white man, waving like the expatriates do.

"Good-em-bye," said the two boys, waving. They watched the man and his carriers out of sight, then turned to walk back to Kati-loma.

"Well, you have walked with the white man, my Sons, and returned safely home to me. Well done, my boys."

Boso smiled as Apa's words went into him, prickling his scalp, tingling his spine and swelling his liver.

"Nogo-Ma was right when she said she would have a son who would grow up to be great like his father. He's starting young, isn't he, Apa?"

"Yes, he has made a mighty early start!"

"I'm so glad I didn't let him be buried alive!"

"I'm thankful too, Son! It took a lot of courage to stand against the whole tribe that day. And it has taken a lot of perseverance and grit and determination to stick to your job and do it right, these many moons. I'm proud of my sons."

"All we want is to grow up to be great like you, Apa."

"You are, Boso!"

"Me, too, Apa?"

"Yes, you too, Dindi. You're already quite a great little man yourself.

THE END

Jacob Mambi aka "Dindi"

Osi Tua in the foreground, with Dindi, aka Jacob Mambi to the right.

Shalom Georgette, Jacob/Dindi's first daughter; Christina, Jacob's wife; and Nora Shenandoah, Jacob and Christina's second daughter.

Jacob Mambi, aka Dindi, with his son, Isaiah, Mendi, SHP
May, 2000

Jacob Mambi, aka Dindi, in his radio station, Nek Bilong Muruk, Radio Southern Highlands, May, 2000

Jacob/Dindi in Wyoming, USA with Linda Pauline
Nicodemus

Linda Nicodemus' grandfather with the wild horse he
caught and tamed, and trained to follow him everywhere,
even into the kitchen. Jacob/Dindi enjoyed this horse and
his trainer. 1984

Hunting deer in Pennsylvania with George Kelley, Jr., Pamela, Bob and Deanie Kelley and Jacob Mambi. 1984

Kanga, aka Carl Mambi,
aka Boso, 2nd February, 1970

Kanga, aka Carl Mambi,
aka Boso, 3rd February,
1970

Tribute to Jacob Mambi on the internet, by a writer
named Daniel:
"After eight years of traveling around PNG and
talking with different radio station managers, I have
never come across such a person of Jacob's caliber,"
says Daniel. "I would describe him as the 'pastor' of
the radio station. He is not just a manager; he is very
strong Christian. When he was a child, he was
adopted by one of the PNG Bible Church
Missionaries (and taken) to the U.S.A. While there, he
completed his communication degree and then came
back to PNG."

Kewa Language Glossary

Ama – mama, mother
Ame – brother
Apa – father, papa
Ere pere naki - last son
giligalas ~ miniature green parrots
Ipa – water
Kaisuwa – grandfather, tumbunu
Kale-nakinu – orphan boys
Kian'alinu – whites, (Literally "Red" – sunburned Caucasians) contraction of
Kianea –alinu - red men
Komea – one, one-fella, wanpela
La – speak, say it. Tokim
Lapo – two, two-fella, tupela
Manda – enough, inap
Malapo – four, foa-fella, fopela
Menda – another, other
Naki –boy, monkey, manki
Nokonaki – child, pickininny, pikinini
Nokonakinu – children, pikinini
Nana – my, mine
-nde – endearing suffix
Ndia – no, nogat
Pawasi – slowly, easy-easy, isi isi
Patepe – you all lie/sleep, Good-bye to those staying
Patepullapape, - you all go sleep, Good-bye to people going away to sleep
Pulapape – you all go, Good-bye to those going
Repo – three, tri-fella, tripela
-si – diminutive suffix
Tapanda - manhouse, haus bilong ol man
Tapa – cloth, bark cloth in particular

Melanesian Pidgin Glossary

Tok Pisin   "Talk Pidgin"

All-the-man! Olaman! Exclamation
Behind-him him. Bihainim em. Repeat after him. Follow him.
Bilum – net bag
Calaboose – jail, prison, kalabus
Easy –easy – slowly, quietly, carefully, isi-isi
Fasten mouse – shut your mouth, (Fasim maus, or Pasim maus.)
Foa-fella – four, fopela (popela, for some who cannot pronounce the English
letter f.)
Fonday – Thursday, Fonde (alternately Ponde.)
Franday – Friday, Frande
Gi – give me
Good-fella – good, nice, beautiful, pretty, pleasing, gutpela

Kaikai – food
Kapomane – government
Kaukau – sweet potato
Kiss-him – bring, take, kisim
Kisim nem – take a census
Karo – car
Kusa – salt
Laplap – cloth (tapa)
Liklik – little
Look-him – look, see, lukim
Monkey – boy, manki
Me-fella – we, us, mipela
Mouse (maus) – mouth
Mumu – (food cooked with hot stones in a pit, in the ground)
Nambawan – Number One, the best, the greatest, etc.
One-fella – one, wanpela
Osi – horse
Pitpit – a cane smaller in diameter than bamboo
Pickaninny – child, children, pikinini
Sararay – Saturday
Singsing – dance
Tainimtok – interpreter, turn-him-talk
Tanket – long narrow leaf, worn as a covering over the hips, by men and boys
Turn-him-talk – interpreter, tainimtok
Toonday – Tuesday, Tunde
Tree-fella – three, tripela
Trinday – Wednesday, Trinde
Tree-fella – three, tripela
Tsimbu – Chimbu, Simbu, a province in the highlands of PNG, or a person from that province
Tsin-fis – tin fish, canned fish
Tsipoon – spoon
Two-fella – two, tupela
Week-time – week, seven days
Wireless – radio
Who's-at – who, husat

Epilogue

Rev. and Mrs. Grover Lytle and family, and a teacher by the name of Marilyn Lavy started a mission station at Katiloma in 1968. Marilyn started the English school, and Dindi was in the first class she began. He excelled immediately as he did in his first two languages. He loved clothes with all his heart and he was not willing to throw away a shirt, even when it was full of holes. That is how I happened to take the picture of him at the end of this story.

He and his three friends were chosen to go to Ialibu High School, where a teacher by the name of Mark Rosen was so impressed by them, that they brought him home to Katiloma to meet us. He became a good friend. Jacob was chosen to become a high school teacher, (secondary school teacher) but he felt God was calling him to preach. Our family took him home with us to the USA when we went on furlough in 1984. The Evangelical Wesleyan Church sponsored him and he attended their school, Adirondack Bible College in New York.

Boso was considered too old for English school when Marilyn started it, so he joined the Pidgin School where he learned to read and write Pidgin, but also excelled so that he was allowed to join the first class in English as an older student and late comer. He did four grades of English, before he got his driver's license and a truck, and became a businessman. He married Ruth Koya in 1971, and had five children, four sons and one daughter, and died of an aneurysm in 1984, just before Dindi's return to Katiloma. Jacob, aka Dindi, married a girl named Christine, from Ialibu and had three children. They settled in Mendi, where he was news translator and commentator for Radio Southern Highlands, Nek bilong Muruk, Voice of the Cassowary.

Mambi was cared for by Boso's widow, Ruth Koya in his last days. Tikira died in 2013, I am told, and this year, February of 2014, Jacob died in the Mendi Hospital. His children and his wife, as well as many others, mourn his passing. I personally did not see him since 2000, but in 2011 I was in Mt. Hagen, when he was in Mendi, but could not come to see me, due to the murder of Boso's youngest son, Donald on police duty, and the wakes he chaired in Mendi. He often called me on the phone late at night though, and we talked at length, and caught up on each other's lives and I was refreshed and cheered by his great personality, his keen insights, and his love for God and people. He was a great man.

ABOUT THE AUTHOR

Linda Harvey arrived in Papua New Guinea with her parents and brothers in January of 1960 when she was thirteen years old. Her parents took five orphans or needy children that year, and when Linda was 14 she moved into an orphanage with four of them, and cared for them with the help of Wameyambo of Piambil and Ellepe of Tona. Wameyambo was fatherless at the time, and Ellepe was motherless. Wameyambo married Stephen Mann and taught at Wakwak School in Mendi for over thirty years. She is now teaching at Kauapena. Ellepe Nomi married Wiwa Korowi, who was later knighted by the Queen. Sir Wiwa Korowi and Ellepe were PNG ambassadors to

Belgium first and he became governor general of PNG. Ellepe bore him three sons, and she is now headmistress of Tokorara Maranatha ACE School. Linda, Wameyambo and Ellepe remain best of friends to this day, fifty-four years later!

When Linda was fourteen and her brother, Jerry, was sixteen, they began teaching the teenagers of Piamble, at the foot of Mt. Giluwe to read and write their own language and count and add and subtract in English. Linda wrote her first two novellas in ImboUngu at that time, and has continued to teach and write, all her life.

Linda married another MK (missionary kid), George Kelley Jr. at Katiloma, near Kagua, SHP, and their first son was born in Mt. Hagen Hospital on 11.11.70. Linda is the mother of three, two sons and a daughter, each married so she has "six kids, just as she always wanted" close to her, and eight grandchildren. She is blessed to be called "Mum" by others as well, including Dr. Peter Yama of Kimbe Hospital, West New Britain Province and Anna Mulu Davis, now of Woodstock, New Brunswick, Canada. When Connie Were hugged her and almost pulled her into her lap, in Mendi, she said in English, "That's okay! You can sit on our legs; you *grew* us!"

Linda was in PNG the year after Jacob Mambi was born, but she did not know him until 1969 when he was in Marilyn Lavy's second grade. Linda is pictured here in 1963 holding Stephen Harvey, a newborn baby her parents took on the fourth of July, 1960.

Linda is the author of six other books and numerous other articles, stories and unpublished manuscripts.

Made in the USA
Charleston, SC
20 June 2014